THE COMPLE
SHOW JUMPER

A training manual for successful show jumping
at all levels

Ernest Dillon FBHS

KENILWORTH PRESS

First published in the UK in 2000 as *Show Jumping for Fame or Glory* by Ernest Dillon and Helen Revington
by Kenilworth Press, an imprint of Quiller Publishing Ltd

This edition published in the UK in 2011

British Library Cataloguing-in-Publication Data
A catalogue record for this book
is available from the British Library

ISBN 978 1 905693 36 8

Photographs by Jim Crighton: (www.jimcrighton.com), Equiscott Photography (www.Equiscott.com), Graham
Gannon: (Image Point Event Photography), Bob Langrish, Brian Potiphar, *Scottish and Northern Equestrian*. The
photograph of Pat Smythe on page 179 was taken from www.cotswolds.info but it has not been possible to trace the
copyright owner.

Line illustrations by Dianne Breeze.
Cartoons by Maggie Raynor.
Jacket and book design by Sharyn Troughton
Printed in China

Kenilworth Press

An imprint of Quiller Publishing Ltd
Wykey House, Wykey, Shrewsbury, SY4 1JA
Tel: 01939 261616 Fax: 01939 261606
E-mail: info@quillerbooks.com
Website: www.kenilworthpress.co.uk

Contents

Dedication

This book is dedicated to my first teacher and life-long friend
and mentor, the late Cyril Johnson, without whom
I would never have lived the life I have.

To Ailsa

Very best wishes

Ernest.

CONFIDENCE!!

:-)

Acknowledgements

Thanks to the following, for their inspiration and guidance:

Cyril and Dorothy Johnson of the Northern Equitation Centre, where it all began.

Robert Hall, Fulmer School of Equitation, who taught me the value of dressage.

Col. Joe Dudgeon, Burton Hall, Dublin, who inspired me to become an all-round horseman.

Elaine Straker, who treated me like one of her sons.

Fred Welch, who taught me how to show jump and earn a living.

Dick Stillwell, who brought me down to earth on a regular basis.

Peter Charles – he should be an inspiration to all young riders who have to start from nothing.

And finally poor Aileen, my long-suffering partner and little Eleanor my beautiful daughter, who keep me grounded.

Thanks also to those who gave of their time and facilities:

Henrietta Forrest for her invaluable editing of the photographs.

Ben and Kathleen Maher, who gave up a lot of time – and their yard hospitality is exemplary!

Mike and Emma Philips from the Quainton Stud.

Bury Farm Equestrian Centre.

Ernest Dillon 2011

Foreword

I STARTED RIDING AT AN EARLY AGE and I was lucky to have very supportive parents to help and guide me on my way. However, no matter how much support and backup I had, I never underestimated the value of good horses, good training and good coaching. Throughout my career I have tried to ride the very best horses I could afford, horses who suited my temperament, my style and my physique.

I have also made a point of seeking out the most successful coaches who were available and spent many hours learning the best and most up-to-date training techniques which suit and enhance the modern sport of show jumping. I was lucky to train with the great Swiss rider Beat Mändli, one of the most stylish and effective riders in the world. He gave me a firm grounding and a simple and effective way of riding which did not interfere with the horse's concentration or ability to jump big and wide fences.

I have known Ernest Dillon for many years and while he is known for his plain speaking and direct approach I believe his knowledge is well founded and his theories simple and uncomplicated. He is an effective coach with quick observation and attention to individual needs and he makes his point simply and clearly. Many riders and coaches do have a habit of overcomplicating and over-theorising, and, although the sport of show jumping is very difficult to master and takes many hours of good practice, it is in essence a simple sport if the simple rules of balance, flexibility, rhythm impulsion and straightness are followed.

The Complete Show Jumper steers the reader along the right path with comparative ease. It sets out a simple methodology and answers many questions which crop up regularly in schooling and training the horse and rider.

Any good coach will have a well thought out and logical system which will avoid confusion and stress in both the horse and the rider. Horses, being the sensitive creatures that they are, will not take kindly to being trained with the stick and sharp spur. It is much better to try to understand the way the horse's mind works and reacts and how his body works mechanically. I believe that Ernest has such an understanding and explains in a very down-to-earth and straightforward way how to achieve a good rapport with your horse.

Ernest's fundamental belief is that, without the courage and mental flexibility to try to learn and progress, success and confidence can pass you by. No one is too old to learn or to improve their technique.

This book will help every rider, whatever level they are competing at, and I cannot recommend it highly enough.

Ben Maher 2011

Preface

WHEN I HAD FINISHED THE FIRST EDITION of *Show Jumping for Fun or Glory* I wondered if I had taken the right approach to what is, in effect, a collection of my own experiences, opinions and methodology. Opinions are very subjective and if I disagree with yours or you with mine, it does not mean that either of us is wrong, just that we differ in them. I have never professed to be a great rider who made a decision to teach, I have always been a teacher who did not ride too badly and achieved what I set out to achieve. I hope that my own experiences should give some hope to less privileged riders who are prepared to get stuck in and have a go. Anything is possible if you use the strength you possess and never give up.

I started from a council house in Liverpool; the only horses I met were pulling a milk or rag-and-bone cart. If Everton were playing at home on Saturday afternoon I might be lucky enough to be hoisted up on a mounted policeman's horse, and once I ran up on to the stage of the Liverpool Empire and got to sit on Roy Roger's famous horse *Trigger*. After that, a fortunate bike ride took me to Aughton Green where my ten-year-old self met the great Cyril and Dorothy Johnston of the Northern Equitation Centre and the rest, as they say, is history.

I was certainly proud of and comfortable with the first edition but everything moves on and many things in sport do change and evolve, so I felt an update was due. Not only did I want to try to give advice on how to train horses, based on 45 years of experience in the equestrian business, but I also wanted to try to solve some common problems and, at the same time, add a little humour to what can sometimes be an over-serious sport.

No one will ever learn everything and certainly the study of how horses work mechanically or how the horse's mind works would take five lifetimes – and even then we would only be scratching the surface.

What I have really set out to do in these chapters is to help readers steer a less traumatic path through the pitfalls of riding and training horses than I had to steer myself, and I hope that everyone who takes the time to read this book will derive much pleasure from a sport which has filled my life. As I have stated many times in the past, I left school at 16 and I have been on holiday ever since.

> The best thing for the inside of a man
> is the outside of a horse.
> (Winston Churchill)

Why Train?

T RAINING HORSES is a work in progress in every rider's life, from Olympic stars to those riding in local unaffiliated shows. There is no end product to training; it is not necessarily competing at a show or being able to jump higher than anyone else in the fastest time. However, performing well at a show is proof of good training. Thus the best-trained horses will jump higher and wider in the fastest time and, more importantly, with the least amount of wear and tear – and so inevitably will win more competitions.

You should not be attempting to win classes at the beginning of your horse's career. His first few shows should only be used to familiarise him with various surfaces, ground conditions, types of show jumps, the atmosphere and the routine of a horse show. Galloping mindlessly around small show jumps time after time will not improve either you or your horse, nor can it truly be called show jumping.

Training of the horse and rider should be a work in progress from which you should diverge regularly, allowing time to compete. Competing will enable you to see if there is a weak link in your training programme, as performing well at a show proves that your training is working. Never forget though, that there is always room for improvement.

Most of the horse/rider combinations I coach are, potentially, much better than they imagine they are; all they need is positive guidance, support and direction. Through correct training even the least talented combinations can achieve things they never thought possible. So how do you go about finding the right coaching, which will result in the sort of training and support you need to jump bigger and bigger courses successfully, while achieving better and better results?

Being in everyday contact with their sport puts professional coaches in a good position to observe changes and keep up to date with evolving modern coaching techniques. They will also be in a position to see, first hand, how the great show jumping riders tackle everyday problems, correct faults and, more importantly, avoid them in the first place.

DAVID BROOME

At no time can you overlook the value of good coaching. Listen to everyone who has something positive to say and glean from it whatever you can. Never stop looking to improve.

Former World and European Champion, three times Olympic medallist and six times winner of the King George V Gold Cup.

Coach's credentials for the job

A good place to start in your search for the right coach is to check their credentials. Qualifications are a good guide and these days, although not essential, they give the rider a feeling that the trainer has taken the time to become accredited and is working in a system that is understandable. Importantly, it also means that the coach will almost certainly be carrying insurance cover. A highly successful competition rider may have the know-how, but may not be able to explain in detail what you personally need, in order to become more accomplished and effective. The opposite also holds true. Someone who may be a very good coach, but who lacks competition experience, can't always see the problem from the rider's perspective.

You need someone in between: a person who is a good and successful show jumping rider but who has a well-thought-out system which they can put across in a simple, easy to understand way. This person may also be a well qualified, accredited trainer. (Accreditation, either to a show jumping, eventing or dressage society, means that person has successfully completed a specific training system that has taught them how to coach correctly.)

Successful work system

A good coach must be able to teach their system of work. Any coach who has not thought through a system will not coach well. Good, successful systems are based, in my opinion, on experience, knowledge and an ability to focus on the individual needs of each horse and rider. I also believe that, to coach well, one needs the ability to keep an open mind and see with a wide-angled lens, rather than with a narrow focus. Narrow-minded coaches tend to miss important points. It must be

POINTS TO PONDER....

If you do it right, it's hard to get it wrong.

A good explanation will put the rider at ease.

Clarifying objectives reduces confusion.

remembered, though, that even the most lucid and far-seeing coach cannot produce more talent than either the horse or rider possess.

Drawing on experience

I also believe that coaches must draw on their own experiences – both good and bad. It is important that the trainer has a sound background of practical experience in the sport being coached, combined with a sound knowledge of generic coaching techniques. That experience and confidence should transfer to the pupil during each coaching session.

Both historian and innovator

A good coach is not only an innovator, but also an historian. Without a thorough knowledge of how the sport evolved it is difficult to move forward with confidence. By this I mean that the ability to compare methods that historically achieved good results with those that were less stylish, less correct and less effective, is an important one.

Goal-setting

It is essential that a coach should be involved in goal-setting. Then, once crucial initial goals have been reached, it becomes a joint responsibility between client and coach through work, discussion and analysis, to set more ambitious, but still attainable goals. I find it is productive to set more than one goal at a time. For example, the achievable goal could be winning a Novice class at the local show in three months' time, while the ultimate goal – perhaps of competing at The Horse of the Year Show – is worked towards more slowly.

The ultimate goal should always be achievable with effort and hard work; it is irresponsible to set an unattainable goal. Aiming *too high* leads to frustration and loss of confidence; however, aiming *too low* can be equally frustrating and becomes boring. Moving someone out of their comfort zone is a very skilful and important part of the coaching process and should be an almost invisible act on the part of the coach. I think the old adage remains true: success by the inch is a cinch, by the yard, it's hard!

Assessing talent

Another favourite saying of one of my own coaches, which still rings true, is that: 'Talent will out', and another fundamental skill of a good coach is the ability to assess a rider's natural talent. By this, I mean assessing the talent the rider is born with; the inherent talent which, in my opinion, cannot be increased. In saying this, I don't mean that other aspects of ability can't be improved upon, through learning good techniques and thus developing each individual to their utmost potential. This has to be done carefully though, as it is sheer folly to push riders too hard or too fast.

Most riders know, deep down, at what level they currently feel comfortable and, when they can accept this, frustrations will diminish. However, while it is the responsibility of the coach to recognise the current comfort level of each pupil, it is also their responsibility to help pupils expand their comfort zones as they improve their knowledge and technique.

With training, success at any level can be very satisfying. My advice to riders is to do what you can do, well. Become stylish and skilful, train to the highest standards and buy the best horse you can afford. If you follow this advice and work hard you will truly develop the talent you have.

Dedication is what you need

POINTS TO PONDER...

Hard work can beat great talent if great talent doesn't work hard.

Both coach and rider have to be dedicated. Dedication is the absolute. Ask yourself whether what you have chosen to do is the right thing for you and whether it is a vocation that you can stick to. I sometimes ask my riders: 'Is there anything that would make you give up show jumping from choice?' There should be only one answer: 'Nothing!' Dedication involves self-motivation, self-discipline and hard work; these are all major factors in ensuring a successful rider–trainer combination. Self-motivation is essential in training. If a rider does not work, with 100 per cent conviction, towards their goal, then no amount of nagging and pushing will create

Begin each session with a simple and basic warm-up.

success. Self-motivation on the rider's part is essential, if their coach is to help them fulfil their talent.

Self-discipline is the partner of self-motivation. An undisciplined trainer will lead to an undisciplined rider, but if the coach is disciplined and sticks to their chosen system, progress for trainer, rider and horse should be smooth. Dedication means training to the limit through hail, rain and snow, 52 weeks a year. Dedication *is* hard work. Dedication is seeing something through without taking short cuts and being able to pick yourself up after a disaster. The road to success is paved with frustration and soaked with sweat and tears!

Coaching qualities – a summary

To sum up – a great coach will:

- Encourage the rider to ride a suitable and compatible horse.
- Have a well-thought-out system and be able to teach this training system in a clear, coherent manner.
- Be able to see all the angles in any given situation.
- Have patience.
- Give confidence.
- Encourage the client to reach an achievable goal.
- Eliminate stress, tension and confusion.
- Create order by prioritising.
- Impress upon the rider the importance of thinking faster to facilitate quicker reactions.
- Look for reasons, not make excuses.
- Accept and share responsibility.

POINTS TO PONDER...

Quitters don't win. Winners don't quit.

Top left: Interaction and feedback are essential with any coaching session. It will help the rider assimilate the information and make the homework easier.

Top right: Group lessons can be a lot of fun.

- Create independence, not reliance.
- Act as a sounding board for ideas and anxieties.
- Encourage the rider to be fit to train and ride.
- Have good communication skills.
- Be constructive, not destructive.
- Listen continually.
- Remember that it is about the client not the coach. The client must have involvement in all aspects of analysing and thinking out strategies.
- Never coach to satisfy their ego. After a successful competition result the coach may well be able to bask in the reflected glory of the success, but that is never the *aim*. The coach must allow the training to be a two-way interaction and must be able to assess their own shortcomings as well as seeing what their clients have to improve on.
- Above all, a coach must be positive in any and every situation.

Remember, though, that the bottom line is that finding a trainer you can trust is still a lottery. You buy a ticket and then hope for the best. When I was a young man – a few years ago now! – I was told that, if something sounds too good to be true then it usually is. So remember, good trainers are like hen's teeth – very rare – so shop around until you find one who matches you and your ambitions.

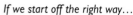

If we start off the right way…

…we will end up the right way!

One of the UK's leading Championship team riders and winner of the Hickstead Derby.

BEN MAHER

Find the best coach that you can: one to whom you can relate – and always be prepared to listen and improve your technique. You can never stop improving.

A light-hearted look at coaching

After all those serious points I thought it would be fun to have a light-hearted look at the world of horse trainers and coaching. Some of these types will be familiar to my more mature readers, while younger ones will hopefully be amused at reading about some of the interesting stereotypes you may come across, once you enter the wonderful world of horse trainers. As times change, some of these great characters may never be seen again and, if only for their wisdom, they will be sadly missed.

The 'feather smoother'

Some riders like to have a 'feather-smoothing' coach; they need to be told constantly how good they are. These coaches are essential to some riders who like to have their egos fed and to be told that everything they do is right and that the horse is always wrong. These riders tend to move frequently from one trainer to another because the last hapless coach eventually slipped up and told them a home truth or two. Such pupils are okay riders, but need to stay secure in their comfort zone and any cage-rattling may cause them to fall off their perch. They definitely need a 'feather-smoothing' trainer.

The 'social life lesson'

Some riders like to go to a coach for more of a social and friendly session, to have a chat rather than to have serious coaching. We all have to become one of these coaches from time to time. These riders like to catch up on all the local show jumping gossip. You know – who's dating whom, what so-and-so paid for their new horse, who was getting merry at the show jumpers' ball and who just can't ride to save their life. That's fine; I like being involved with these 'lessons' now and again, because it keeps me up to speed with the gossip as well and it's light relief during a hard day's work.

These riders attend lots of shows and know all of the top riders 'really well'. They tend not to compete much themselves, but get someone else to ride their horse: 'Just to freshen him up!' Sometimes they walk with a limp at shows, the reason being: 'I got bucked off yesterday and I can't ride for a week.' They do, however, limp around the show in the latest equestrian designer gear.

The military man

I love these guys; retired Majors and Colonels from the old cavalry regiments, they sport highly polished brown boots and always have a moustache twinned, more often than not, with a pipe stuck permanently in the side of their mouth. They have a voice that could stop a charging horde and a biting, sarcastic sense of humour that can reduce even the most hardened pupil to a tearful, dithering wreck.

For many years, this was the only style of coach there was and no one expected anything else. These were, after all, men who had survived the Normandy Landings and they had no time for wimps or whingers. Some, I have to say, got results – albeit

by the stick rather than the carrot. Riding whip tucked under arm; hands behind their backs, bow legs and baggy breeches, their philosophy was that to succeed you had to want to win. The idea that winning isn't everything did not enter their heads and the opposite of a winner is a loser. Even a good loser is still a loser. These old-school trainers weren't interested in one-off moments of glory, or one-day wonders. During training sessions they expected buckets of sweat to be dripped from riders with sticks under their arms, jumping down lanes, first with no stirrups, then without saddles or even bridles.

One of my most memorable quotes was from a certain Colour Sergeant of the Royal Scots Greys: 'There's two ways o' doin' things, the reet way an the wrang way and you lads an lassies'll be doin' it the reet way!' Oh they were the good old days!

The Pony Club teacher

These trainers are all, without doubt, heroic. They are often volunteers or else underpaid. Undervalued, overworked and jolly to a point that astounds me, they roll up to rallies and shows in all weathers. They bear the brunt of the bickering, in-fighting and jealousies of all the Pony Club mums, dads, sisters, aunts and uncles, all of whom are far more competitive than their little princes and princesses. They have to teach people on all kinds of unfortunate animals, from the small child on the enormously fat pony, who can't trot more than one lap without risking a heart attack, to the skinny girl nearly 6ft tall who won't part with her outgrown 13.2hh event pony. From the rugby-loving, hulking great teenager on his dad's 'mouth like iron' hunter to the 15-year-old princess in her designer bling, who has a great deal of talent for attracting hormonal polo-loving boys, but sadly, not for riding.

LIVING THE DREAM!

Of course, there is also the odd, dedicated young person wishing to learn; serious riders who haven't much of a chance among all the rest of the attention seekers. Amazingly these trainers always seem to turn chaos into some kind of order and are still smiling at the end of every day.

Johnny Foreigner

For a long period in the UK we had the idea that any trainer who spoke with a German, Swedish, Dutch or French accent would automatically know far more than a trainer with a well-educated Oxbridge English accent, let alone a provincial one. This, of course, was because 'Johnny Foreigner' was trained in the appropriate *haute école* and knew all about the mystical world of 'dressage'. Besides which, someone losing their temper in a European accent always sounded far more impressive, especially if they also lapsed into their native tongue from time to time. Comments like: *'Gut ja'*, given at least 40 times in a lesson made you feel really…*'gut ja'*. The trainer, in turn, felt extra *'gut ja'*, when you merrily handed over a cheque for three times what your home-grown trainer would dare to charge.

What we all aspire to through correct training.

I am not suggesting for one minute that these guys were not (and are not) very good, but there is still something very fashionable and chic about talking about one's trainer, Heinrich, François or Count von Vasterglutton, at the pre-event cocktail party.

The newly qualified teenager

We all know one – hard hat, gloves, two sticks, three pairs of spurs of different lengths, made-to-measure boots, spray-on breeches, and a new certificate from some obscure college in the back pocket, which tells everyone they are a manager and fully qualified teacher. I think that these guys are great; they can

name every muscle, every ligament, bone and tendon in the horse's body – but have no idea how they work. But heck, ain't science wonderful? They have little black books full of the names and addresses of the very best physios, chiropractors, masseurs, farriers, saddlers and horse dealers, all of whom will help you ride better. They have also 'read all the books' and know all the terms necessary to sound incredibly knowledgeable. They might even come out with the odd: *'Gut ja'*. Ah youthful enthusiasm!

WILLIAM FUNNELL

Never lose track of the basics. Every successful rider establishes the basics in every schooling session. Without a good foundation you cannot progress.

Three times winner of the Hickstead Derby and Super League team member.

Choosing and Obtaining a Show Jumper

MY KNOWLEDGE of what type of horse makes a good show jumper comes, not from any great experience in the breeding industry, but from my experience as a user and a trainer of the end product. Over many years I have trained a great many horses and, without doubt, the easiest type of horse to train is the quick, sharp-witted, quality horse who is flexible in his body and has a mind he's happy to put to work with me, rather than against me. Horses of this type can start off their career being difficult to manage, but this is only because they have quick minds and, as we all know, a quick mind can pick up bad habits just as fast as it can develop good ones.

It is a common misconception to think that, if a horse is well bred, he will have good conformation and that, if he has good conformation, then he will have good technique and movement. Unfortunately this is not always the case. If a horse has a severe conformational defect, causing a fundamental weakness in his movement, this will become magnified under the stress of competition and you must consider whether such a horse is usable and for how long.

However, some of the world's best horses have had defects that would not have passed a meticulous vet; one who springs to mind was David Broome's *Mister Softee*. He had sickle hocks and looked weak in his hind legs and very bandy from behind, but he won an Olympic bronze medal in Mexico in 1968 over one of the biggest show jumping courses ever seen; he was also three times European Champion. On the other hand, I have spent many frustrating months trying to turn perfect-looking show horses into show jumpers, with no success. There was no apparent reason why these horses could not jump but it was obvious that they had neither the enthusiasm nor gutsy determination to try. Provided the quality comes out somewhere, whether in the stride, the jump or the brain, the old adage 'handsome is as handsome does' rings true.

Having said that, the modern-day show jumper has to be much lighter and considerably faster than those of the past, both across the ground and in the air,

CHAPTER 2

NICK SKELTON

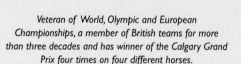

You need a good horse – that's the most important thing. When you've got the best horse life becomes a lot easier, but good horses can be incredibly difficult to find.

Veteran of World, Olympic and European Championships, a member of British teams for more than three decades and has winner of the Calgary Grand Prix four times on four different horses.

plus have a very scopey and careful jump. He has to have the ability and confidence to think for himself. Self-reliant horses will be able to deal much better with the complicated technical difficulties of the modern show jumping course. They will also be well equipped to be careful over the lighter materials used to construct the jumps nowadays. The show jumping world has embraced the importance of good blood lines and, consequently, there are many more horses being bred for the job and therefore it is much easier to find the type of horse suited to the rigours of a long jumping career.

Conformation points to look out for

There are some structural defects that are likely to reduce the working life of a show jumper dramatically and there are some features that I particularly look for when buying a horse. Here is a guide that may help you when choosing your show jumper.

A horse with severely upright pasterns is going to have less absorbency in his fetlock joints, so I do prefer a horse to have sloping pasterns. A large proportion of lameness in show jumpers is caused by concussion and jarring of the feet and joints. Good feet are essential to allow for some expansion and movement; the old saying, 'No foot, no horse', still holds a great deal of truth. When a horse lands over a jump, all of his weight will come into one foot; that is about 600kg (1,320lb) of horse coming down on to an area of about 100 square cm (16 sq in), a huge amount of weight on a small area.

A good, long, sloping shoulder is important. Straight shoulders cause more

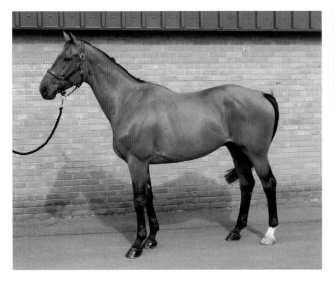
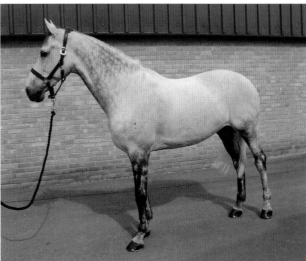

jarring and straight-shouldered horses tend not to be very careful, because of their inability to rotate the shoulder and bring it up in the correct way.

Two good examples of a modern quality show jumper.

I tend to be attracted to horses with smallish, quality heads and big, bright, alert eyes. I will not buy a horse who has what I can only describe as a 'dead eye' – and by that I mean an eye that has no expression and looks asleep even when the horse is in work.

A well-muscled back of good proportions is great but I have no strict rules here – long- and short-backed horses have made superstar show jumpers throughout the sport's history, as have sway-backed and roach-backed horses. I can't think of

A really bright, intelligent head with a bright, bold eye and a great outlook.

A bold, brave outlook showing intelligence and courage.

A kind, sensible head which will inspire trust and confidence in any rider.

any great horses who had cow-hocks or spavins, but I have already mentioned *Mister Softee's* sickle hocks – and the legendary *Ryan's Son* had large curbs.

Good and correct technique is also a point of much discussion between professional show jumpers. If you consider all the world-class horses and mark their technique out of ten, against the classical description of a good jumper, none is likely to reach a perfect ten. John Whitaker's great grey horse *Milton* (the first horse to win a million pounds in prize money), used to unfold his forelegs in mid-air and pushed his feet way out in front of him, over the highest part of the jump. Classicists would dismiss him as being short of scope, saying that he was reaching for the back rail! Marion Mould's great pony *Stroller* (at 14.2hh, a legend in his own lifetime), was a silver medallist in the Mexico Olympics and winner of the Hickstead Derby, yet he used to jump fences any way he could and seldom the same way twice. Malcolm Pyrah's ride *Anglezarke* jumped in a slightly inverted manner, with his head up and his neck hollow rather than rounded. But all of these horses shared one great quality: they had a burning desire to leave fences standing. These slightly freaky horses are not so common these days but they do pop up from time to time and cannot be ignored.

Suitability

Many riders, when they go to buy a horse, have a good idea of what they want and of the type of horse they would like to ride in the ring, but that horse may not be the most suitable type for them. What tends to happen is that they either find themselves over-horsed, in terms of size or temperament, or just totally mismatched in terms of temperament, type and ability. It is difficult to explain to

A really good example of a native pony x Thoroughbred: a 148cm (14.2hh) pony suitable for any discipline, with an ambitious young rider.

A solid native pony, like this traditional Connemara pony bred in Ireland, will give a junior rider a great experience and a tremendous feeling of confidence.

someone just embarking on their show jumping career that suitability is one of the most important factors to take into consideration, and not just a horse with a huge jump.

Most people should start their show jumping career on a good schoolmaster type, maybe a good quality cob type or an older horse who is steady in his mind. This is not the big, thickset, lumbering horse that people automatically imagine when the word 'cob' is mentioned. An Irish Draught x TB makes a good type to begin show jumping on. He is likely to be alert and agile enough to go to the fence and jump correctly, but will be sensible enough not to rush or do other crazy things. This doesn't mean that, with some years of experience, you can't upgrade to higher-quality horses with added scope. This first type may be a more difficult horse to find, with the huge influx of continental Warmbloods, but they can be a pleasure to ride and have extremely reliable temperaments. I would say that if you are comfortable within the first ten minutes of trying a horse and you feel safe, then follow your gut instinct.

Imagine going to Ascot or any other Thoroughbred Bloodstock Sales and buying yourself a horse straight off the racetrack, bringing him home and saying: 'This is my new show jumper.' If you have little or no experience of training, or more particularly, retraining, then you are going to dig yourself into a very deep hole! Young horses who have had a bad start or have been trained only to gallop are best left to professional producers and even they will have a hard job with such animals – their success rate is very low.

One thing that is important to point out is that when you start out on your career, you should not jump straight on to the kind of top-quality, athletic horse you see jumping in the Olympics, the Hickstead Derby or at the Horse of the Year Show. To be honest, if you did jump straight on to such a horse, you would be more likely to scare yourself to death! If I were to present you with a top-flight show jumper you would probably ask me to take him back within a week, not because he was not a good horse – he might be the best, most multi-talented horse who has ever lived – but because he would not have been suitable for you. You would hardly recognise him as the equine genius he might be with a Marcus Ehning or a Ben Maher on board – and not because you are a bad rider, but purely because you are not suited to one another. Good horses certainly do make good riders but, like a good husband or wife, they have to come along at the right time for you to take advantage of them.

At the beginning of my career I was lucky enough to have a very careful little horse called *Davy Jones*. He had tremendous talent and used to hate hitting fences; the trouble was that he was much better than I was. I had not yet recognised or realised my talent, nor did I have the experience to do him justice. He came along too early in my career and neither of us fulfilled our potential together. We were both too young and too inexperienced to make a great partnership. Sure, we did

How I wish I had him now –
the author and Davy Jones.

win quite a few classes together, but not as many or as prestigious as they should
have been – I wish I had him now!

Ninety per cent of riders are essentially recreational riders; they jump for fun
and they try to get as much enjoyment out of show jumping as possible. To get that
enjoyment they need a good-tempered horse who is easy to train and is going to
be reliable and not too unpredictable. You do have to be realistic about the amount
of scope and jump that you need. A high proportion of people who are looking for
an International level show jumper, really need a top-class Riding Club horse or
schoolmaster, capable of jumping 1.10–1.25m (3ft 7in–4ft 2in).

Either you or your coach should know at what stage you are with your show
jumping and you should have an idea, albeit a vague one, of how much talent and
potential you really have. You may not always be the best judge of your own
temperament, talent and progress, but you should be able to place yourself
somewhere, in the great scheme of things, as a show jumping rider.

Nearly everyone wants to spend as little money as possible. Horse prices
change from year to year and bargains can be found, but most people purely want
value for money. This is very simple to equate: if you pay an amount of money that
you have judged to be reasonable and your horse does the job that he has been
bought for successfully, then he has proved to be value for money. If you pay the
same amount of money and end up with a horse who does not do what you want
him to, then you have not had value for money.

If you don't have a bottomless pit of money or the sort of talent that it takes to
jump International Grand Prix courses, then you are looking for a happy, honest
and fairly brave little trier. A good guide is – if you are riding to a fence that is big
enough for you and you feel that your horse wants to get to that fence at least as
much as you do and then, when you get there, your horse clears the fence and

Beware of a horse with a sense of humour!

lands in balance, despite your usual number of missed or panicked strides and he repeats this a dozen times and still feels happy – then it is likely that you have found just the right horse for you.

The show jumping horse's brain is a cocktail of courage and caution. The cocktail has to be mixed in the right strength so that whoever is drinking the cocktail can cope with its potency. Too much caution makes a horse too careful. He will not want to hit fences but, if he does, he will not want to try again. He will very quickly become stressed and will start stopping or napping and not wanting to go to the fence. The problem of having an over-careful horse can be overcome, to a large extent, by making sure that the competitions he is entered in are well within his scope and that he is ridden by a competent, accurate and experienced rider. He will need a lot of time and patience but the finished product will be a delight to ride and, having gained the confidence in his good rider, he will try over and over again.

On the other hand, too much courage in a horse is not conducive to winning classes either. Such horses do not disregard hitting fences but are sometimes unaware that they have done so. They appear to have an overdose of adrenalin or, perhaps, an insensitive mind. Often they seem much braver than they are because they seem happy to keep running at fences. Horses like these are difficult to win classes on, even with good jockeys, but brave horses ridden by novice riders can give the rider a great deal of confidence, even if the occasional fence comes down. There is nothing worse for the novice rider than to be eliminated at the first fence or to have a horse who is 'hiding in the corner', too afraid to come out and perform, or one who is jumping up and down on his hind legs, refusing to go forward.

What most of us try to obtain is the horse who is the most difficult to find: one who has a high degree of both courage and caution; one brave enough to go to his

POINTS TO PONDER...

Buy a horse you can ride.

fences, yet careful enough to jump them well and leave them up. Though not easy to find, this is not an impossible dream. If it were, then there would not be so many good show jumpers in the world today.

I do not have all the answers to trying to find a horse who will suit you, but what I can do is to point out some of the pitfalls you might encounter and advise you how best to steer around them. Over the years I have fallen into the snake pit many times (every professional has – that is how most people become good judges of horses) by buying and trying to ride a whole bunch of bad and unsuitable horses. Horses cannot help it if they have little or no talent, or if they are not as brave or as careful as they should be, any more than a person can help it if, through bad upbringing or lack of direction, they find themselves in the law courts too often, or if they have two left feet when on a pair of skis.

I have bought horses from many different types of dealer and have had a great deal of fun meeting some of them. Below is a cross-section of dealers I have come across.

The lighter side to buying your Olympic dream

This is the really fun bit…or not, depending on how it turns out. When you declare out loud that you're in the horse-buying market, oh boy, watch all the vendors crawl out of the woodwork.

The private seller

Sometimes private sellers are genuine and honest. And sometimes they may not be. For example, sometimes the seller is simply a parent who is selling a child's pony who has been outgrown. Or, maybe the parent is selling because:

- The child is going to start college and the parents need money for tuition fees.
- The child has grown up and finds that boys or girls are more interesting than horses. (Very common.)
- The child has lost his or her nerve, after a fall. (Be suspicious.)
- The child is doing poorly in school and the pony is a distraction. (Bet the poor child doesn't think so.)
- Dad has lost his job so there's no spare money for a horse. (Sad.)

There are more reasons for people wanting to sell their horses than I could write in half a dozen books. Some are genuine and others are not. When buying from a private home it's important to follow your gut feeling and hope that your gut is having a good day. Let's also hope that you're a good judge of character.

Of course it's nice if you know the people; maybe they're in the same Riding Club as you, or you've seen the horse or pony at shows. A full set of ribbons, rosettes and cups is a pretty good recommendation. But it's a pretty good price-booster as well.

If you haven't seen the horse or pony at shows then maybe the seller can show you videos of him competing. Beware the conveniently edited version. You know, where the knock-down, refusal or fall, is skilfully wiped from the footage – not difficult in these high-tech days, most five-year-olds can do it.

Some private vendors may also allow you to have the horse for a trial period, but this does require a huge act of faith on their part. They are taking a risk, as there is no guarantee that the horse will return to them in the same condition that he left and, for the period that the horse is away, no other potential buyer can view him.

The horse dealers

These come in all shapes and sizes. For example:

The old farmer

He's dressed in welly boots, greasy, baggy trousers that are held up by baling twine and he has a set of bow legs that couldn't stop a pig in a passage. He has an old tatty coat and a flat cap, a cigarette hanging out the side of his mouth and there seems to be more hay and straw in his hair than there is in the stable. But don't judge by appearances. This may be an old stereotype of the dodgy dealer but, strangely enough, these guys probably have a nice type of horse tucked away somewhere, and are generally very honest people.

I suspect he might have been a great horseman in his day and just sells a horse or ten to help in his retirement. Judge for yourself by the reactions of his horses and his manner around them.

I know an old chap in the north of England who fits this description to a tee. He has 40 horses in his paddocks from foals to eight-year-olds, from untouched to just broken. He goes by the name of Oliver and I can't understand a word he says. But he'll let you try anything you want and spins you no yarns. He knows all the breeding of all his stock, from great-grandma down, and has little idea of their value. He is a great guy.

Flash Harry

He appears dressed as if he just stepped out of his office. He wears a Savile Row suit, camel overcoat and a trilby hat. His shoes are shiny and he may even have a flower in his buttonhole. This guy drives a Mercedes or Jaguar with a personalised numberplate 'NAG 1'. He looks as if he has never ridden a horse in his life and he probably hasn't. Yet this dealer's great talent is

that he can talk the hind leg off a donkey and make every word sound believable. If he says: 'This has never happened before!', as you're lying under the jump, looking up at your prospective purchase, be wary.

This dealer talks out of the side of his mouth and mumbles so that you're a bit confused about what was said and when. He doesn't look you straight in the eye when he tells you his horse will never stop, nap, buck, rear, bolt, weave, box-walk, bite or kick and, in fact, will jump over the moon if you ask him to. His horses don't need to jump over water, they could walk on it!

Flash Sally

While Flash Harry looks as if he just stepped out of the office, Flash Sally looks as though she stepped out of a magazine. She's usually very pretty and is wearing loads of make-up; she has perfectly manicured nails and nice breeches. She knows all the tricks of the trade and can spin fairy stories to fit any occasion.

Flash Sally is the female version of Flash Harry, but the main difference is that she'll

have spent a lot of time in the saddle and will have the horse ready for you to see. The horse will put on a great show and be turned out to perfection. His mane and tail will be plaited, feet polished, tack clean and shiny; the stable will be well mucked out and the stable yard swept to within an inch of its life.

The horse she shows you may be great or not, but trust me, get the same warranties as you would ask for from any other dealer.

The professional horse producer and breeder

The horse producer either breeds and rears horses, or starts, schools and competes them, with the goal of eventually selling them on. These people may be men or women, old or young, but they all have one thing in common: they like their horses and only buy what they like. You're pretty safe with such people because they rely on their reputation and repeat business.

They'll also try hard to fit the rider with the horse because they do not want you to bring the horse back, if he doesn't suit. You will be almost 100 per cent safe with such dealers. If the animal they sell you doesn't work out, it will more likely be by mistake rather than by intent. Try to find these dealers by recommendation via word of mouth, as they hardly ever advertise.

Taking advice from experts

So, you have found a horse to try, but who do you take with you for advice? Beware the expert; these people also come in all shapes and sizes and their job is to help you, the buyer, find the right horse or pony…and maybe grab a bit of commission on the way. But they are not all bad.

The newly qualified teenage expert

These experts have learned everything there is to know about the horse world by the time they are 17. They will tell you that they have ridden since the day they could walk and sometimes before. They're well turned out: designer jeans and made-to-measure chaps complete with frills; highly polished boots and well-ironed shirt. The jacket they wear will almost certainly bear a logo, advertising their show jumping/eventing/dressage team. Alternatively, they may have just graduated from an equine college and have a crisp new certificate on the bedroom wall.

You will know these guys because they will carry two whips, one jumping and one dressage; they also have a crash helmet, back protector and gloves in their car at all times (just in case). They might talk a good story, but look out if they don't want to ride the prospective purchase – what if the guy who is selling it puts up a fence that's higher than 76cm (2ft 6in)? Also beware if they run around the countryside with you for weeks, turning down loads of horses, but then show up with a horse or pony belonging to themselves or their best pal – for twice the price – that's perfect for you.

The very old expert

These experts are the exact opposite of the teenage one. They will have spent a lifetime with horses and ponies, yet may never have owned a particularly good one. They probably had lots of pet horses – maybe even a hunter or two. They will have attended tons of seminars and lectures/demonstrations given by real experts and will have a hat-full of quotes. They will have attended more Pony Club rallies than you have had hot dinners. The main problem here is that they'll be slightly out of touch with modern-day requirements for a competition horse. Sometimes these poor old folk will not even be able to see the horse very well at more than a few steps away and, if you get bolted with, bucked off or dumped, it will be because the 'jolly splendid animal is just a little high-spirited'.

The real expert

Now these are real experts in their particular field – jumping, hunting, dressage, eventing or showing – and they are the people to ask advice from. They've been, or are, highly successful competitors in their field. Or they're highly successful coaches and trainers, with vast amounts of experience, advising mums and dads on the right pony for their children. They come in all shapes, sizes and ages and two things they have in common are a wealth of knowledge and a background of making successful purchases for themselves and their clients. They will not embarrass anyone by taking you to look at unsuitable animals, nor will they waste your parents' time and money.

So what's the problem? The top professionals charge for their time and advice. Of course, you and I know that a purchase this important is worth it. If mum and dad ask an experienced, successful person to find the right horse for you from the beginning, it will save thousands in fuel, vet fees, medical bills and, possibly lawyer's fees, trying to return unsuitable purchases.

Down to brass tacks

Horses can be bought from breeders, dealers, high-performance and bloodstock sales, local auctions or by private sale. Most amateur riders buy their horses through advertisements in national magazines or local newspapers. Yet this can be the most time-consuming and frustrating way to purchase. Everybody within a 100-mile radius has got just the horse for you! Perfect in height, weight, colour, breeding and temperament: careful, scopey and brave; has never stopped or napped, is easy to catch and has never shown the slightest inclination to bite, kick, buck, rear, weave, crib or box-walk. He is in fact, a paragon of virtue.

In fact, when you arrive to view said paragon, he is a hand and a half shorter than stated and rushes at you with bared (but worn down) teeth, then turns on a sixpence, letting free with both barrels, before rushing off to the other end of a large field, never to be seen again! If you do manage to catch and ride him, everything he does wrong, from refusing, napping, rearing, bucking or knocking down fences, will be greeted with the declaration: 'Oh, that's the very first time he has ever done that.' How many times have I heard vendors state that categorically?

Another pitfall of buying through an advertisement is that you can never be sure who is doing the selling – whether it is the horse's owner, the owner's agent or an undisclosed dealer. The sale of horses is, to a certain extent, covered by the Trade Descriptions Act but should you need to resort to such means of redress, the procedures can be expensive, time-consuming and sometimes, acrimonious.

To get serious, it is important to find out about the horse's past. A sample of questions to ask might be:

- How long has the present owner had him and why is he for sale?
- How long has he been doing the job for which you intend to use him?
- What successes has he had?
- Has he hunted?
- Is he safe out hacking on roads, alone and in company?
- Is he good to box, shoe, clip, catch, and groom and with strangers, such as the vet or the dentist?
- Is he suitable for the type of rider you are? Here you have to be honest with yourself. If you are quite a nervous or novice rider you should tell the vendor.

If the horse you are going to view is registered with an affiliated body, then you can obtain a record of his jumping successes. Check the record for long gaps and question the vendor about these – it is possible that the horse was either injured or went through 'a difficult spell'. All of this information can be gained by a telephone call and can save a lot of time.

Once you arrive to see the horse you need to give him a fair trial. First, you need to see him ridden by somebody else and then you need to ride him yourself. Never offer to get on straight away – a strange horse is an unknown quantity and may just be waiting to get you off, in any way he can. If the owner assures you that he is good in traffic, ask to see him ridden along the road – you might follow behind in a car.

As the horse is being bought for the purpose of show jumping, don't forget to try him over a variety of fences. Put up double and treble combinations, as you are likely to jump them in competition. You are never going to be in a better position to do so and it is no good getting halfway home and suddenly thinking that you should have tried this or done that. If the horse is being bought to event make sure that you see him jump a couple of solid fences, a ditch or two, and going through water. If he is very green he may have problems with these obstacles, but you should be able to gauge his attitude and temperament.

If there are no such facilities at the vendor's home, ask if it is practical for the horse to be taken to a venue where there are plenty of coloured fences, including a water tray and solid fillers, to try him over, unless he is a young, inexperienced horse. The vendor may huff and grouse but that's tough; it is your money and it is up to you to ensure that it is well spent. As long as you are fair to the vendor, you are entitled to a good trial. On the flipside, it is completely unfair to waste people's time. As soon as you are sure that the horse will not suit you, say so – politely. It is very irritating to vendors if you start picking holes in the horse – he may not suit you, but somebody will buy him and will probably be very happy to have done so.

Sometimes you may see the horse loose-schooled. If done in a professional manner this will give you a good idea of the horse's natural ability and it will certainly tell you if the horse cannot jump. However, carried out by amateurs, the whole project can quickly turn into a shambles. You end up watching in bewilderment as the vendor tries to loose-jump a poor green-as-grass young horse. People will be tripping over themselves and their lunge whips trying to impress you with their horse's gymnastic talents, making pretty big fools of themselves. Of course, you do not offer to help because you can't see the horse performing properly if you are running around waving your arms about, but the real reason you do not offer to help is that you do not want to spoil the entertainment! More seriously, this is not a good way to see the horse go and when you go into these yards and see this sort of thing happening, it is more embarrassing than anything else. You came to see a young horse showing his talent, not to see him being frightened to death and running away from a lot of hollering, whip-cracking handlers.

Buying from dealers

Buying from dealers can be a very successful way of buying the horse you want. There are 'dodgy dealers', people who have a reputation for knocking poor or bad horses into shape and getting rid of them, but most dealers rely on having a good reputation and on getting business through return trade and recommendation. As mentioned earlier, good dealers seldom advertise and you will hear about them through word of mouth.

Dealers may not know very much about the history of a horse but they are in the business of selling horses for profit and tend only to buy horses they think are good enough to sell on in the first place. Dealers build their reputation on selling the right horse to the right person, so they are unlikely to sell you a horse unsuitable for your ability or intended purposes. Some, but not many, good dealers will offer you a short trial period during which you may return and exchange the horse if you experience problems.

Sales

If you wish to buy a horse from a sale you should ensure that he is sold under warranty – that he is guaranteed by the vendor to be sound and free from vice. It can be quite useful to see several horses together so that you can compare their various merits and shortcomings and you can also manage how much you spend – as long as you have strong self-control!

At high-performance sales you can see horses ridden and jumped, usually by a professional rider, but at markets or auction sales there is a very limited amount of access to a horse in terms of a trial. You can look at him, feel his legs and gauge his temperament; you may be able to see him trotted up or even be able to ride him at the pre-sale viewing day. The drawback with this is that he may have been ridden by a few riders that day and so not show his true ability or temperament.

If you are taking an adviser, make sure they are working for you and that they know what you are looking for. It may not be intentional but sometimes, through inexperience, the adviser may put you off buying a horse who would suit you. You must be sure that the adviser is entirely familiar with your experience, ability and requirements and also has sufficient knowledge and experience to make a true and sensible judgement. Although you may have to pay for good advice from a professional person, you are far more likely to end up with the right horse than if you enter this minefield unaccompanied.

Ultimately, remember to see the horse stood up and trotted without tack; see him ridden on the flat and over fences (which are fair test of his honesty and ability) before you ride him yourself. Try to be as objective in your opinion and judgement as possible and remember that first impressions are very valuable. If your gut feeling tells you that this is the horse for you, he probably is! Conversely, if something seems too good to be true, then also it probably is.

Get him vetted

Whether you buy a horse from an open sale, a private vendor, a dealer or even from a friend, you should have him inspected by a veterinary surgeon. If you already use a vet in whom you have confidence, then ask them to vet the horse for you. If the horse is a long distance away then ask your vet to recommend one in the horse's locality.

Most veterinary practices will offer to perform either a full, 'five-stage' vetting or a 'part' vetting. A part vetting, although obviously cheaper than a full five-stage one, is usually little more than a visual observation of the horse, standing and trotted up in a straight line and is really not worth the financial saving made. If you intend to insure the horse for 'loss of use', then you must opt for the five-stage vetting anyway. This is a very comprehensive vetting which usually takes about

Two examples of really spectacular technique and every rider's belief: 'Give me a good horse who tries his best and I can win competitions.'

an hour and a half and includes taking a blood sample. The blood is usually stored for six weeks but is not usually analysed unless you are worried that your horse was slipped a Mickey Finn at the time of purchase.

The perfect horse has yet to be born, so tell the vet what you intend to do with the horse so he or she can gauge whether or not any lumps, bumps or conformational defects are likely to affect his ability to perform for you. The important point to remember about a vetting is that, ultimately, the horse needs to be usable for the purpose required of him. *Usability is a good word to remember.*

Starting the Young Horse

THE ADVANTAGES of buying a young, unbroken horse are that, so far, nobody has taught him bad habits, training him can be both satisfying and rewarding and such horses tend to be cheaper than horses already in work...but why? Simple – it takes months of hard graft and skilful training to produce a horse who is already working well under saddle; and hard graft and skilful training cost money. The disadvantages of buying a young, unbroken horse are that – guess what? It takes months of hard toil and skilful training to produce a horse who is ready to work well under saddle! If you do decide on a young horse and want do things yourself, then read on.

For a start, although I have used the term 'unbroken' above because it is the term commonly employed, the expression 'breaking a horse in' is not actually one I like. It seems to suggest the breaking of the horse's will, when the reality is that we are trying to make the horse accept us and carry us while submitting quietly to our will. Many modern 'horse whisperers' would have us believe that their way of starting horses is the only kind way to do so and that, until they came along, everybody was doing the job incorrectly, but I believe that, with some unsavoury exceptions, horses have been started humanely for hundreds of years.

That said, I have a huge amount of time for ideas and the innate feeling of the horse whisperer – I think many are very fine, naturally talented people with a good rapport with horses, but I believe starting horses is a progressive task. From halter training through to International competition jumping, there has to be a systematic approach and follow-through. I am not happy with the idea of chasing a horse around an arena for ten minutes, putting a rider on his back and saying that he's ready to go – go where? What tools does the horse have to understand his rider and to be obedient?

I believe wholeheartedly that what a horse learns in the first six weeks of training, he falls back on for the rest of his life, just as a child at primary school remembers what was taught in those early days for the rest of his or her life – namely the ABCs. If you don't teach your horse his ABCs in a correct way then he is going to grow up with no clear concept of how to behave. I have been lucky enough to work with some superb horsemen in my life and every one of them has said that you need time when you are starting horses. It is no good trying to train a horse in five minutes and to expect him to stay trained. Nor can you lunge your youngster on Monday, then leave him in the field until Friday and expect him to remember anything.

Starting a youngster takes planning

When starting your youngster you have to be with him every day: handling, grooming, lungeing, once, twice or even three times a day if his temperament requires that amount of input, to instil in him a sense of routine and discipline. For this reason, think carefully about the time of year that you start. If you work from 9 to 5 you ideally want to start training your youngster in early summer so that you have enough daylight and time ahead of you to do the job properly.

I like to start horses when they are three years old because I think that young horses are much more pliant, inquisitive and more open to suggestion than older horses. They are also willing to learn, have a better attitude when it comes to accepting and absorbing knowledge and have a better memory. I don't like starting horses younger than this because their tendons and muscles are still developing and their bones are still soft.

I feel that starting a horse is best done by a professional and, now that I am too busy teaching to spend a lot of time with a youngster, I send my young horses to another local trainer to start. To find the right place to send your youngster, ask your instructor or knowledgeable friends about good yards in your area. Starting horses is, in my experience, not the province of young, rash or inexperienced people; it is best done by older, experienced people who are strong-minded yet patient and placid. Such individuals have usually assisted experienced trainers before starting in business themselves.

Checks to do before sending your youngster away

Before he goes to the chosen yard, ensure that your horse is up to date with his tetanus and flu vaccinations, is wormed and has front shoes on. Your horse's first shoeing may be an eventful, even traumatic experience if he has had little done to his legs or feet before. This trauma may be reduced if you handle your youngster's legs and pick his feet out each day. If you have older horses, tie your youngster next to them each time they are shod so he gets used to the sounds and smells of shoeing.

Ask a vet or an equine dentist to check his teeth. Rough edges or wolf teeth (small teeth sometimes found in the upper jaw in front of the molars), can catch painfully when the horse has a bit in his mouth and will quickly make him afraid of it. Wolf teeth have no purpose and are easily removed by a vet or dentist and sharp edges can be rasped off. Finally, I like to have my youngsters checked by a physiotherapist to ensure that there is nothing glaringly wrong with their back musculature.

Doing it yourself

If you are determined to start your young horse yourself you need to have a willing, competent lightweight helper, plenty of patience and at least a couple of spare hours each day, for the next six weeks or so – consistency is the key to success. When you educate your horse you must be calm and quiet but you must also be firm. I do not speak down to children – I do not say: 'Coochy-coo, where is the woof-woof and where is the gee-gee?' I say: 'Where is the dog and where is the horse?'

Similarly, when I am talking to horses I do not talk down to them, I talk to them in the language that they have to learn to understand. 'Walk on', means the same thing to a horse whether he is three or 23 so, within reason, you can afford to teach the young horse in the same way that you teach an older one. You do not approach the subject of teaching a young horse to walk, trot and canter on the lunge, under saddle in any different way than you intend to carry on his education at a later stage.

Young horses being started are going to buck and squeal and do all kinds of things in the same way that young people do: young people buck and scream and make nuisances of themselves, but you have to put up with it. In fact, if a young horse doesn't show some form of rebelliousness, I will worry whether his disposition is strong enough for him to do what I want him to do. I like a horse to play and fool around a bit and show a bit of character. It is important that you don't punish your youngster for minor misdemeanours or for showing high spirits but let him work them out of his system naturally. Move slowly, talk quietly in a low voice and remain patient; bad temper never won a battle. Horses get used to laid-back, easygoing people far more quickly than they get used to sharp people who are always on their case, so it's good to be very quiet.

Equipment

The equipment you will need consists of a snaffle bridle, an old but serviceable saddle, a lunge cavesson and two cotton webbing or leather lunge reins (*not* nylon), a roller with a breastplate (this need only be a length of baler twine), exercise boots, overreach boots and thick gloves. Cracked leather, worn girths and weak lunge lines are a recipe for disaster and you will end up hurting somebody – this will seldom be you because it is not you who is climbing on; it is your assistant. Other than the saddle, make sure that everything fits your horse well before you start. As your horse develops, his body will change shape, so you need not buy him a saddle that fits him perfectly until he is in regular work. In the meantime use a numnah or thick pad to make sure the saddle you use does not pinch or rub him. (This does not, of course, mean that it's okay to use a saddle that is a *rank bad fit* – anything that hurts the horse or interferes with his movement will not endear him to the idea of wearing a saddle.)

Have all the equipment you are going to use ready, in the right place at the right time before you start. It is no good taking your youngster down to the field to lunge, only to find you are missing a side-rein. This is not only frustrating for you but also for your horse. It is lovely if you have all the best facilities, such as an indoor school, but we do not all have these so most people start young horses in an enclosed space like an outdoor manège or small paddock. It is important to consider the facilities you have carefully before you start. If, for example, you start your horse in the middle of winter and it is pouring with rain and you haven't got an all-weather surface, you are rapidly going to run into problems.

Getting started

Start by lungeing your horse with just a cavesson, lunge line and whip. In order to get him moving forward you have to walk a little behind him. In the beginning, ask your assistant to lead him from the outside on both reins until he is happy to move forward around you. If your assistant can lead him for the first five or six circuits for three or four days this will be a great help, otherwise just continue to stay a little behind your horse, driving him forward on to the circle.

The lunge whip is not a weapon – it is your leg aid when you are on the ground – and should be used in the same manner, effectively and with skill. If you ever start beating your horse with the lunge whip then you have lost and that is sad. Your horse will start to become whip-shy and will run away from the whip and from you. Once he starts to run away from you, you have lost his attention, he will panic, his instinct for flight will take over and all he will be interested in will be getting away from you. The whip has to be used effectively by showing it to the horse behind him and by giving him a light flick above the hocks when necessary.

Always wear gloves when you lunge to avoid rope burns as these are painful and unnecessary. A young horse is almost guaranteed to rebel and run off from you at some point and, if you are not wearing gloves, the pain of the lunge rein whipping through your hands is likely to make you let him go, with possibly dangerous consequences. I would also advise you to wear a helmet, as a kick in the head can do massive damage.

Continue for three of four days, teaching him to stand, walk and trot on command. Use the same word all the time for each command, whether it be 'Walk' or 'Walk on', 'Trot' or 'Trot on', 'Whoa', 'Stand' or 'Halt'. Use the tone of your voice to indicate the need for a change of speed or gait. When you are asking your horse to move up a gait, make the command brisk and upbeat and when you are asking for a decrease, use a calming, soft, lower tone.

If your horse's circles are more egg-shaped than round, use the lunge whip moved forward towards the shoulder to keep him out. You can also use eye contact and body language to drive him out. If he pulls out, use a give-and-take contact on the lunge rein to encourage him to become lighter in the hand. You must watch your horse's body language so that you can be one step ahead of him. If he attempts to whip round you must be there before him, moving back towards his quarters and driving him forward again.

Put the bridle on after the first or second day but continue to lunge off the cavesson. If your horse is lungeing well after four or five days, you can put the roller on him. This is an important thing to get right. Initially, you cannot girth your horse up tight enough to prevent the roller from moving backwards. If you put the roller on without any form of breastplate it is likely to end up around the horse's backside and he will buck like a mad thing. You don't have to own an expensive breastplate – even a piece of baler twine as mentioned above will do – anything to keep the roller in place. (The first time you put a roller on, don't be surprised if your horse bucks to begin with, as the experience of something constraining his middle is alien and not very pleasant.

Once he is comfortable in the roller and is moving forward confidently on the lunge you can introduce the side-reins, loosely at first but, within quite a short time, tight enough so that you are driving your horse into a contact – much as you would if you were riding him. I prefer elasticated leather side-reins with buckles which are easy to adjust, stay in place and are reliable, however nylon side-reins are okay – just make sure they are elasticated and are adjusted equally.

Within ten days of starting your horse he should be working happily on a circle on the lunge line with side-reins on, walking, trotting and standing to command. Now is the time to introduce the saddle. Use an old saddle to begin with, so that if the worst does happen, you have not ruined your best competition saddle. Again, you will need a breastplate on and an assistant to hold your horse. Initially, just lower the saddle on to the horse's back a few times, so that he can adjust to the extra weight. Once he is comfortable and relaxed, put the saddle on and girth it up gently but not too loosely as you do not want it ending up between his legs. Next, attach the side-reins, take his head, and ask him to walk on in the usual manner. The chances are that when he feels the tight, hard saddle on his back he will have another fling; that is fine, but do be ready for it and when he has finished, ask him to move on in walk and trot. At this stage you can also fit a loose standing martingale – the neckstrap may come in handy to hold on to later.

When your horse is working happily in the saddle and the side-reins, you can start to introduce the second lunge line around the haunches and then begin to long-rein him off the bit. Nowadays I am in the minority in driving horses in long-reins but I do have a problem with the idea of getting on a horse that I cannot stop. I think it is ridiculous practice that the only tool you have to help you stop your half-ton, three- or four-year-old horse, when you get on his back, is to say 'Halt' or 'Whoa'. If he doesn't want to listen I like to have a bit of back-up and if the horse has never learnt that increased bit pressure means stop, then he is not going to learn the instant I get on top.

More advanced work

The Irish horse-copers call it 'putting a mouth on a horse' and what it means is, teaching the horse to have some kind of obedience to the rein. My horses halt, walk, trot, turn left and right and change the rein on the long-reins. In fact, by the time I get on them, they can work in the long-reins much as they would if I was sitting on their backs.

Long-reining is a great but dying skill. There are many ways of long-reining but my preferred method, in the absence of a fancy roller with lots of rings, is to tie the stirrup irons together under the horse's belly, using a spare stirrup leather, and to pass the outside rein through the stirrup iron behind the haunches and back to my hand. The inside rein passes through the inside stirrup iron and comes straight to my hand. Be careful when bringing the outside rein around the haunches, as your horse is very likely to lash out with his hind legs, until he becomes used to the pressure of the rein.

Soon, your horse will be lungeing confidently on both reins and can change the rein whilst still on the outside circle. I have travelled miles and miles on the lanes and bridlepaths long-reining young horses; getting them used to traffic, dustbin bags and pushchairs. We will walk and trot, halt, rein-back and be gone for hours. I do realise that it is not possible to long-rein horses in the middle of suburbia but it should be possible, with the help of an assistant, to find some quieter roads on which to long-rein and accustom the young horse to traffic.

Backing

At this point you should have been working your horse for about three weeks. If he lunges on both reins in a saddle and side-reins, and you have long-reined him and he appears confident and happy with what he is being asked to do, then now is the time to start backing him. Everybody seems to have a different system for backing a horse but I back mine in the stable. They are in familiar territory, relaxed, confident and happy. Logically the horse is less likely to perform badly in his own house than he is in the middle of a large field.

You will need your assistant at this stage. The fitter, younger, lighter and possibly less experienced person is the person who needs to get on the horse. The more experienced person should always be on the ground. You do not need the younger person holding the horse and the poor old codger (like me) getting on, as that is a recipe for disaster. Strength is not important but the experience, confidence, reliability and horse-sense of the person starting the horse is. What is important, however, is that the person getting on the horse is sensible, quiet and totally sure of what they have to do before you ask them to do it.

At first give the jockey a gentle leg-up, inching them higher and higher until they are leaning lightly above the horse's back (now you know why the jockey should be light). The jockey can then talk to the horse and pat him or stroke him along his neck and on his flanks. Then the jockey can be gently lowered back to the ground while continually talking to the horse. Leg-up the jockey from both sides until the horse is thoroughly at home with feeling someone above him. You can do this for two or three days, leading the horse around the stable to the left and right, until you are sure the horse is relaxed and happy before letting the jockey sit on his back.

Once the horse is fully confident about somebody leaning over him in the stable you can repeat the same process in a manège or field. Eventually your jockey can gently ease a leg over the horse's back and come into an upright position, still talking to the horse all the time. You, on the ground, should slip the jockey's feet into the stirrup irons. Once the jockey is on board, staying there is very important, so every effort should be made to avoid any possibility of being bucked off – hence feet in the stirrups.

Walk the horse around the manège with the jockey holding the reins in one hand and the pommel in the other. With very few exceptions, the horse will accept the rider's weight very quickly. If your horse begins to buck and squeal, stop and talk quietly to him and then send him forward. The jockey will hopefully not fall or jump off as this is more likely to frighten the horse than anything else. When the horse is moving well around the manège on the lunge, both you and your jockey can ask him to halt then walk on as he has learnt to do before. Gradually the jockey can begin to put pressure on the horse's sides and to steer the horse with the reins.

The scary bit comes when you put the horse back on the lunge and ask him to trot on. Usually he puts his tail between his legs and scuttles off but if you have him on a fairly short rein and the jockey is prepared, the latter will just move with the horse and wait for him to settle down into a rhythm. The most terrifying thing to happen, from the jockey's point of view, is for you to let go of the lunge at the critical moment. There is nothing worse than a loose lunge line whipping around the horse's legs as he plunges to and fro in a panic. For the jockey the best thing to remember in that situation is stay on top if you can – it's safer up there!

Now five or six weeks into your horse's training, he is getting used to the rider taking charge whilst on the lunge. He is obedient to the rider's requests to walk, trot and halt. He has not cantered yet, as I do not believe in cantering horses on the lunge when they are being started.

When he is off the lunge, you should be introducing the horse to new experiences, rather than keeping him in one field or manège. I think that young horses learn very little from trotting round and round in endless circles but they need to develop strength, character and balance, in a straight line. In other words, they need to learn about life. Always take him out in company and be positive, sensible and firm – even tough if necessary (*tough* is okay but *rough* is never acceptable). If your horse stops and looks at something, reassure him, give him a pat and allow him to go past in his own time. If he stops and spins around and is misbehaving, straighten him up and give him a slap with the whip just behind the leg. Although your reaction to misbehaviour must be virtually instantaneous, it should be well considered. Think about on which side of the horse the whip should be used to be most effective and be prepared for the horse's reaction – don't catch him in the mouth if he leaps forward which is, after all, the direction in which you want him to move. Once he behaves, give him a reward such as a kind word and a pat. Weak riders teach horses bad habits.

I think it takes eight to ten weeks to start a horse correctly, giving him time to adjust to each new stage of his training and to develop an in-depth understanding of what is being asked. A very important point to remember, throughout your horse's training, from starting to setting out on the Grand Prix circuit, is to plan. Plan a training schedule of what you are going to do each day, week or month. When you set your schedule you should have a clear vision of what it is you are trying to achieve on each particular day. If you have no particular goal and are riding around in aimless loops then you do not have a good training programme. If you are specific and plan every step according to your horse's progression, then things will advance a lot more quickly and smoothly.

A horse who begins his schooling in the manner I have described will stay calm, level-headed and confident and, in time, he will develop the trusting nature needed to become a competition horse. Every horse is entitled to a fair start and if he has one he will carry on his life in a good way and he will be respected.

Working your Horse on the Lunge

Why lunge?

CHAPTER 4

WHY DO WE USE THE LUNGE? Many riders think of lungeing as a lazy alternative to riding, the: 'I can't be bothered to ride today, I'll just give him half an hour on the lunge' syndrome, but correct lungeing is a very useful tool for schooling horses. I use the lunge for two reasons, the main one being to break down some of the resistances encountered while schooling and to develop the horse's top line of muscles. It is very easy to lose your patience when you are sitting on your horse and he is not doing what you have told him to do.

There may be any number of reasons why your horse is not doing what you want him to do but to get into a big argument with him will get you nowhere. Horses are not people and sometimes they will behave badly and sometimes the answer is not to be found from on a horse's back. It can be easier to get off your horse and see if you can solve your problems through lungeing. This is not to say that every time you encounter a problem on your horse you should get off and lunge him instead, so that he is allowed to get away being disobedient, but rather that, if you feel that the problem is not going to be solved from his back, then see if you can solve it on the lunge.

The second reason why I will use the lunge is for fittening work. You may not own a horse-walker or be able to ride for as long as you would like, and lungeing can 'top up' your horse's work level. You can even teach a less experienced person to lunge your horse in an effective way, therefore releasing you from daily riding, although you need to understand that teaching a person to lunge in an effective manner does not equip them with the knowledge to 'school' the horse on the lunge. However, less damage is done by inexperienced people lungeing, than by inexperienced people trying to ride a fit competition horse.

Equipment

The tack we use is very important. I came across a clear example of this a few years ago when a world-renowned trainer was giving a lecture-demonstration in front of a large audience, including me. He was intending to give an insight into his method of lungeing but was using a strange and, unbeknown to him, young horse. He tacked up the horse using a saddle, snaffle bridle and set of draw reins (tucked under the stirrups), all perfectly acceptable equipment to use on a horse known to you. Unfortunately, this particular young horse had a slightly suspect temper when it came to being restricted and the upshot was that the horse panicked, ran backwards, reared and landed up in the laps of the audience. Thankfully nobody was hurt but the trainer and everybody watching learnt a useful lesson – know your horse before you do anything with him.

The lunge line is much more effective when attached to the bit. I attach the line to the bit on the outside ring, pass it up over the horse's poll and thread it though the inside ring of the bit, to my hand. This gives much more control over raucous horses and gives a small amount of poll pressure, encouraging direct flexion. However, a lunge cavesson is good to use on young horses during starting. It puts no pressure on tender mouths and offers more control than a headcollar.

Schooling the horse well on the lunge is just as difficult as riding well, although it requires different skills. There are many different reins that you can use on the lunge but I use just four.

The Pessoa system

This relatively modern system of lungeing the horse was devised by Nelson and his son Rodrigo Pessoa and it encompasses everything that is good in training: acceptance of the bit, engagement of the hind legs, development of the top line muscles plus flexibility and balance.

The rein can be attached in three different positions: between the horse's forelegs to develop and encourage full stretching over the back, to the middle of the roller to encourage a natural head-carriage and to allow the horse's neck out and forward, or to the 'hand' position, on the top of the roller, to develop collection and produce more 'push' from the hind legs.

As with any system of lungeing, the experience of the trainer is of paramount importance. The ability to assess progress and an eye for the correct usage of the horse's muscles is something only experience will develop in the trainer.

I usually recommend five minutes on both reins, in the stretch position; five minutes on each rein in the middle position and a further five minutes on each rein in the collected position. Also, of real value, is to go back to the stretch position for five minutes to conclude the daily programme.

The horse working in the 'stretching' setting on the Pessoa system.

The horse is now working on the 'side-rein' position; here it is obvious how much more engaged and 'uphill' the work is.

Here the horse is working in the 'hand position'; this picture illustrates the ultimate engagement on the lunge in canter.

As the horse develops his strength and balance, canter work can be introduced and gradually increased. I recommend that the bulk of the canter work is done using the rein on the middle and upper positions. It takes massive strength in the horse to canter correctly in the stretch position. Another, more advanced technique with this system of lungeing, is to use raised trotting poles to encourage more elevation in the step; this should only be used with the middle setting to give maximum benefit.

Working on the Pessoa rein twice a week will enhance any work programme, but ideally in addition to, not instead of, riding.

The Chambon

Another useful and effective piece of equipment to employ on the lunge is the Chambon. It was designed purely for use on the lunge and is, in my opinion, dangerous to ride in, as there is no release mechanism. The equipment is simplicity itself. It is attached at one end to the girth then splits into two reins and comes up through the horse's forelegs, before dividing either side of the horse's neck. Each rein passes through rings either side of the horse's browband and is attached to a snaffle bit.

If the horse raises his head, gentle pressure is exerted on his poll, thus he is encouraged to develop a low head-carriage. This enables him to stretch and bend though the whole top line of muscles and enables him to swing through his back. Your ultimate aim, when using the Chambon, is to have the horse's head and neck long and low, just above the ground. It is not there to force the horse into submission but to suggest, by slight pressure, that a rounded shape should be adopted.

Its value is that it encourages the horse to use his head and neck to balance himself by lowering the head towards the ground, thus developing strong top line muscles evenly on both sides. The horse releases himself through the back and can use his hind legs more effectively to propel himself forward more actively. Once your horse has come to accept the Chambon he will work in a comfortable, relaxed way, swinging through his back and engaging his hocks evenly.

Even the horse with a naturally low head-carriage will benefit greatly from working in a Chambon. His ability to use his back will allow his hocks to come more underneath his body and redirect his balance to create a higher head-carriage and a more controllable horse.

To be effective the Chambon should be used on a regular basis. Younger horses should be lunged in a Chambon three times a week and some of the older horses can be lunged in it every day. This, again, is in addition to being ridden, not instead of it. It is never necessary to use the Chambon for more than 25 minutes a session (younger horses need only between 15 and 20 minutes).

When you tighten the Chambon, ensure that you do so by small degrees; to increase the pressure on the poll too quickly may panic your horse. As he feels the resistance he will try harder to raise his head and, as the panic sets in, he is likely to run backwards, possibly sitting down on his hind legs or falling over. Panic on the Chambon is, however, rare as long as the horse is aware of what the rein does and it is only tightened gradually. I find that it usually takes six or seven periods on the lunge using the Chambon for horses to understand the rein's effect and for them to start dropping their head and continuing in a calm manner.

The result of lungeing in a Chambon, apart from stretching and creating flexibility, is that as long as the horse is kept active he will develop exactly the right muscles for show jumping. If you look at the shape of a horse using a Chambon you will see that he has his withers and shoulders up, his head and croup down, his hind legs pushing forward and his back as round as possible. Because there is never a direct pressure on the horse's mouth there is never an opportunity for the horse to lean on the rein or pull against the bit.

Draw reins

I prefer to use draw reins (attached to a roller) rather than side-reins on the lunge, my reason being that the side-reins can be too inflexible and can set the horse's neck in a rigid, immovable position, and show jumpers need to be able to move and use their necks and backs in both up and down and sideways movements. Flexibility and strength are two key words in the horse's physical development and one without the other is of no use.

As with the Chambon you should only tighten the draw reins slowly, noting your horse's reaction to the new sensation each time. If he looks a little worried – if his ears start to go back, his head starts to shake or he becomes tense through the back – then go back a stage and loosen them off a hole. The aim is always to allow your horse to find his way in balance and outline and for activity to be encouraged, not to force him into a specified shape and then chase him. Submission to the rein is your primary objective but submission that comes gradually will last a long time. If you force the horse into submission it will only cause resentment and possibly panic and will give you a major long-term problem.

Side-reins

I am in no way against side-reins but I feel that they can be difficult to adjust and can create more problems used badly, than they can provide benefit used well and, unfortunately, I have seen them used badly more often than well. As with all reins, the horse should move forward into the contact to create acceptance in his mind, rather than the rein pulling the horse's head in. Pulling his head in will only result in the horse finding a way of evading the pressure by dropping behind the bit and tucking his head into his chest. Eventually his brain will start to think backwards and he will not want to move forward at any time. Again, adjust the reins slowly, by degrees, but always making progress.

Jumping without a Rider

ONCE YOUR HORSE IS HAPPY and confident being lunged on the flat you can begin to think about the benefits of jumping on the lunge and loose-jumping. The one thing both forms can most definitely do, is tell you whether or not your horse 'can' jump. It is very useful to observe your horse from the ground so that you can see what technique he has and what part of that technique needs developing or correcting. For instance, if his shape is wrong over the fence you could lunge or loose-school him over wide, low oxers or, if he is a little careless, you could loose-jump him over some small, short-spaced gymnastic fences, one-stride doubles or even some small bounce fences. For safe distances see Jumping Combinations, Chapter 12. If your horse has been jumping badly when ridden, but jumps beautifully when loose-schooled, take a careful look at yourself and your tack – something that is perhaps seemingly innocuous to you may be a source of severe discomfort to your horse.

Whether you are teaching a horse to jump loose or on the lunge, you have a similar objective – that is to teach him to take care of himself and to find his balance without the interference of a rider. It is important that your horse is allowed to come to the fences in his own tempo, be that trot or canter, without being chased.

Whether you are jumping on the lunge, or loose-jumping, it is important to have an assistant to build and rebuild the jumps.

Loose-jumping

Loose-schooling will be difficult unless you can find an appropriate area in which to do it. If you attempt to loose-jump in a vast field you will spend more of your time running after your horse than jumping him; conversely, if your paddock is too small, your horse will be falling over himself trying to scramble around tight corners and jumping on his forehand.

However, if you have an area of about 20 x 40m, loose-jumping is an excellent exercise for your horse. If the arena is outdoors you need a substantial boundary fence and if there are any mirrors around the arena these may need covering up so that your horse is not tempted to run at them thinking they are an extension of the arena. It is important to create a jumping lane to prevent your horse from turning around or running out. Of necessity the lane has to be constructed substantially higher than the fences to be jumped, but not so high that your horse can run underneath it. It is simple enough to do this using jump stands and poles.

The trick of loose-jumping is never to chase your horse fast into a fence that is too big for him. To crash into a fence, causing hurt, fear and loss of confidence, is the absolute opposite of what we want to achieve. Loose-jumping is used to develop confidence and technique and should be carried out in a controlled, calm and stress-free environment.

One problem you may face is trying to find enough suitable people to help. Your assistants need to be fit enough to keep up, not aggressive or awkward, and need to be in the right place at the right time. Two assistants are ideal, one to send your horse on down the lane and one to keep him straight down the lane. Ensuring that your helpers know where they should be and what their task is before you begin means the session will be constructive and is less likely to end in tears. When loose-jumping make sure that you are always in the right place. If you are too far in front of the horse as he starts down the lane, you are likely to head him off and he may turn back, yet if you are too far behind him, you will seem to be in a chasing position and he will run away; so stay on a line just behind the horse's hocks and use a lunge whip as a visual aid rather than a physical one.

Another good idea is to round the corners off with poles at about 1m (3ft 3in) high. This will help the horse to run around the corners rather than into them, where he may stop and refuse to come out. Get your horse relaxed and used to running through the lane over a pole on the ground. Progress from there is very straightforward as long as you don't frighten your horse by chasing, shouting, whip-cracking and by building unsafe jumps. Remember to loose-jump on both reins or you will develop a horse who can only jump off one leg.

The purpose of loose-jumping is to teach the horse to think for himself and to promote good judgement and self-reliance, not to see how high or how wide he is capable of jumping. Its benefit is only maintained while your horse's confidence grows. There is nothing more beautiful than a horse jumping free over a substantial fence, but it's neither necessary, nor useful, to turn a loose-jumping session into a Puissance competition. I cringe when I hear people boasting that their three-year-old can jump a 1.60m high by 2m wide (5ft 3in x 6ft 6in) oxer – just how many jumps has a horse got in his life and what is the point of wasting those jumps for vanity's sake?

Jumping on the lunge

I prefer to see horses jumping well on the lunge rather than loose. As I have said, you need a great deal of skill to lunge on the flat and you need extra skills to lunge a horse over a fence. Again, the set-up for jumping on the lunge is important. You must make sure that the lunge line cannot get caught or snagged on anything and cause the horse to get a bad jerk in the mouth. I use the lunge line as described before, threaded from bit ring to bit ring over the poll, giving more control, but this also means that you have to be very careful not to catch your horse in the mouth at any time, especially mid-jump. If you do so he will become inverted or he will start to turn in mid-air and lose his balance.

You need to ensure that your horse can't run past the fence on either side so I use running rails on both sides of the fence. The wing on the inside of the fence needs to be low enough so that you can easily let the lunge line slip up over the running rail and over the wing without you having to fling your arm and the lunge line into the air. The maximum height for an inside wing would be 1.30m (4ft 3in). 'Jumpkins' or 'Blocs' are excellent substitutes for a traditional wing, although with Blocs it is handy to fill them with sand or gravel so that they are not so easy to knock over. Running rails need to cover any place where the lunge line might snag.

Both lunge jumping and loose-jumping should be used sparingly and only on good going, never on sticky, slippery or hard going, as this will destroy rather than build confidence. If you use these forms of jumping to help your schooling rather than to replace it, then both you and your horse will reap the benefits.

On Board – The Rider's Position

AT THE BEGINNING OF THE TWENTIETH CENTURY, Federico Caprilli, an Italian cavalry officer, watched the new wave of flat-race jockeys and realised that this method of riding would benefit the jumping horse. Up until then, riders had been encouraged to lean back as the horse took off, to lighten the load on the forehand. Caprilli devised a method of riding over fences which allowed the horse enough freedom to negotiate the obstacle with as little interference as possible. The simple basis of this system was that if the rider's centre of balance remained over the horse's centre of balance, the horse would have more freedom of movement and thus be able to clear much higher and wider obstacles without endangering either man or horse.

To achieve an effective, balanced position you should fulfil the following criteria:

- You should remain in balance with the horse throughout the approach, take-off, flight, landing and recovery phases of the jump.
- You should remain independent of the rein and, under no circumstance, interfere with the horse's mouth over the jump.
- Your centre of balance should remain in harmony with your horse's centre of balance; there should be no sudden or unnecessary movement of your upper body to distract or unbalance the horse.
- Your lower legs should remain close to the horse's sides, strong and immobile throughout the jump.
- Your weight should be light on the horse's back.

If you aren't sitting correctly on your horse, nothing you do will work. The foundation of the modern jumping seat is a strong lower leg position. Without this it doesn't matter how you sit, because as soon as the horse moves, you will lose your position. The lower legs should stay in the correct position while you are

This young rider is in perfect harmony with her horse – note the sympathetic automatic release through the arms.

taking off, in the air, and when landing. That is not to say that they can't move a *little* backwards; there are very few riders who can maintain an absolutely perfect position throughout the jump – especially over very high, wide obstacles – and there are several riders at the top level whose legs do slip back a little habitually; this (which is very different from the aerial acrobatics of some riders from the past) does not stop them from being very effective.

Years ago, if you could hold a five-pound note between your knee and the saddle as you rode, then you were considered great. However, the problem was that knees clamped to the saddle act as pivots, causing the lower legs to swing backwards and the upper body to swing forwards, putting the rider's weight on to the horse's shoulders and making him heavy on his forehand. This is not good when you need a show jumper to be ultra-light on his forehand with all his power generating from his hindquarters.

The lower legs should be underneath the rider with the stirrup leathers vertical. The knees, far from being clamped to the horse's sides, should be more relaxed and can even be held slightly off the saddle, to enable the lower legs to be kept close to the horse's sides. The toes, which were once expected to be turned to the front

Correct stirrup length and effective leg position – note that the stirrup leathers are vertical.

Short stirrups = a strong centre of balance.

If you ride with long stirrups your body is more likely to pivot out of balance.

Mirrors are a great aid to help you with your position. Don't be modest!

and parallel with the horse's sides, should be positioned at about ten-to-two and the heels should always remain lower than the toes. This light, balanced seat gives the rider a solid foundation for maintaining a strong and well-balanced jumping position over the fence, perfectly in harmony with the horse's movement.

The type of horse you are riding, combined with experience and personal preference, will govern whether you should sit lightly on the saddle with three points of contact, or up out of the saddle on the approach to a fence with only two points of contact. I teach riders to adopt the light, balanced, forward seat as an exercise at any level and especially when they first come to me for training. I firmly believe that riders learn to ride better when they are taking their weight in the forward, two-point position, out of the saddle, and then develop the position in the saddle at a latter stage. It develops their sense of balance and rhythm without having to use their seat at all. Consider that both Flat and National Hunt jockeys spend most of their time in races without their seat ever touching the saddle and observe their wonderful sense of balance and rhythm. As their horses move underneath them, the jockeys shift their weight to remain in balance with the horse.

UK International Team Manager.

ROB HOEKSTRA

“ It is really important to remember the basics. Position is everything in any form of equestrian sport. You need to have a good position to be able to control your horse; to make him go forward, to stop and go left or right at exactly the right time. Position is everything. ”

A turn in balance with the rider in the two-point position.

Another example of the two-point position with the rider galloping at speed.

A turn in balance with the rider in the three-point position.

The forward seat (or two-point position)

The forward seat derives all its strength from two fundamental, irrefutable facts. The first is that the lower leg position is directly under the rider's body with the stirrup leathers vertical and the second is that the angles of the hip, knee and ankle joints allow the rider to find a point of balance whilst the horse is in motion.

The upper body position derives all its strength and stability from the angles of the hips and the knees. In this position, 50 per cent of your weight will be in front of the knees and 50 per cent behind them. How you distribute your weight on top of your horse will greatly affect his way of going. The essential thing is that your weight should be even, in front and behind your knees. Too much weight to the front will make you top-heavy, throwing your horse on to his forehand; too much weight behind the knees and you will get 'left behind', making you hang on to your horse's mouth to keep your balance.

Balance during riding is not *static* but *dynamic*. Because the horse is always moving and his balance shifting it is important that you always follow his motion and do not get left behind. If your hips and shoulders are already in position, the balanced seat allows you to be still on the take-off – no extra movement is necessary. Your head should be up and looking in the direction you are going.

There is no absolute formula for the forward seat and different horses respond to different weight distributions. In some cases the seat may be just fractionally out of the saddle, whereas in others the horse will go better if the seat is up to a full 15cm (6in) out of the saddle.

There are many exercises that you can do to assist the forward seat and improve your balance. Working on the lunge allows you to work with no reins or stirrups to help you develop a sense of balance and position. The most common mistake that riders make nowadays is to ride with their stirrup leathers too long. Up to a point, the shorter your stirrup leathers, the easier it is to find a point of balance. A good guide is that the angle of your knees should be approximately 90 degrees.

The hands should be carried just above the withers. Some horses need to be ridden on a longer rein, while some riders need to ride with a longer rein. If you a have short arms it is very difficult to ride with a short rein. The position of the rider's hands has to correspond with the conformation of both horse and rider. The hand, through the reins, can be used in three different ways:

1. **The direct take and give on the rein**, in which the hand and elbow are being drawn back to the body.
2. **The open rein**, in which the hand is moved away from the horse's neck (a good rein to use on a young horse and in a jump-off situation to ask the horse to start to turn in the air over a fence).
3. **The indirect rein**, in which the hand is actually going across the horse's neck. There is little use in show jumping for the indirect rein, but it can be used to encourage an increase in the left or right flexion of the horse's neck.

Other elements of position

Soft hands and elbows

At this point it is helpful to give you an idea of what to do with your hands when the horse is jumping. I am always aware of my elbows; it is important to keep a good connection with the horse's mouth through soft elbows. This does not mean loose reins; it is possible to have 1kg (2.2lb) of pressure on the rein with a fixed elbow, or with a soft elbow. Of course, a soft elbow is far more acceptable to the horse's mouth. So far as allowing the horse to use his head and neck over the jump, perhaps the easiest and most straightforward method to learn is the 'crest release'. This can be either long or short.

This rider is using arms as opposed to wrists to complete the turn. Elbows are a valuable aid to the show jumping rider.

Before I continue with this explanation, it is important to state that we are aiming at the arm's movement being entirely natural and automatic throughout the jump.

The long crest release involves the rider's hands being placed on the horse's neck some 15–25cm (6–10in) in front of the horse's withers. The action of the release enables the novice rider's horse to jump without hindrance and the rider to stay in balance using the horse's crest to stay in position. I would add a caveat to this, that using any kind of release is only effective after the horse has left the ground. Releasing the contact in front of the fence is tantamount to losing the horse's balance.

The short crest release is the same as the above, however, the hands will only move 5–8cm (about 2–3in) forward; riders will need to be a bit more advanced before being encouraged to use the short release.

So, to reiterate, perfection is eventually achieved when the rider is in perfect balance and thus able to follow the movement of the horse's head and neck automatically throughout the jump with soft arms and elbows.

Here we can see an approach at speed. The horse has taken off a little far from the oxer and the rider is using the crest release to good effect.

Look up

Because your head is the heaviest (one seventh of your whole bodyweight) and the least flexible part of your body, the most important thing is to keep it still, with your eyes looking up in the direction you are going. Once your head drops forward or to one side it starts to influence the balance of the rest of your body and thus the balance of the horse.

Core stability

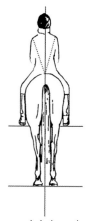

The rider who tips forward will put too much weight on the horse's shoulders and forehand and will also have an unstable lower leg position. This rider will be unable to develop power from the horse's hindquarters.

This rider is in balance: weight travels directly down the spine, through the seat and stable lower legs, into the heels.

The rider who tips backward puts too much weight on the horse's loins and will tend to get 'left behind' as the horse moves off. This rider will eventually cause the horse to become stiff and resistant through the jaw, neck, shoulders and spine.

(a) The correctly balanced and positioned rider's weight is central in the saddle and equal in both stirrups.

Riders' backs can get rounder over the years if they never take the trouble to develop good *core stability*. What is this? Core stability is simply the development of the core muscles in the abdominal region of the rider's body – not just the development of a glorious six-pack but the deep muscles we can't see and which hold our body erect and stable, including the lattisimus muscles through the back.

There are many ways to develop good core strength and stability but the best and most effective method for the rider is simply to develop correct posture on the horse's back and, in developing this, to become flexible with the horse's movement i.e. for the rider's movement to blend with that of the horse. If you allow your back to sag, the rest of your body becomes weak, which will affect your ability to control both yourself and your horse. If you are in a good position in the saddle, you are in a good position to control your horse. A good idiom to strive towards is: 'erectness without stiffness, suppleness without slackness'.

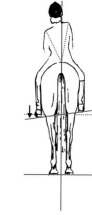

(b) The rider who is out of balance, with weight unevenly distributed over the horse's back, will unbalance the horse. The horse will, in time, become sore and stiff. In this illustration the stiffness will particularly affect the nearside, where most of the rider's weight is deposited.

Stay still

In riding over jumps the aim is to keep all unnecessary movement down to a bare minimum. This has two purposes, the first being that the less movement you make, the more able your horse will be to listen to the intentional movements you *do* make, so that he will be better equipped to respond to your aids. I liken this to two people talking to each other: if they are in a room on their own they can talk quietly and still each hears every word the other says. However, if they are at a party with loud music playing, they not only have to shout, but each is likely to miss words. Try, in your riding, to keep the background noise down to a minimum! The second reason for keeping your movement to a minimum is to prevent your horse from being thrown off balance by sudden shifts of weight.

As I pointed out earlier, if you are already in the two-point position you should, in principle, remain in the same position throughout the approach, take-off, landing and when moving away after the fence. If you are approaching the fence in a sitting position, you will need to close the angle at your hips as your horse leaves the ground, but never throw your weight forward as this will only put your horse off balance and on to the forehand – the cardinal sin of show jumping. More fences are knocked down because of this sudden movement from the rider than from clumsiness on the horse's part, and more refusals occur for the same reason than from the horse's disobedience. A reminder is to think that all great riders are a split second behind their horse and that all bad riders are a split second in front of their horse. The aim is to lower the centre of balance toward the horse as opposed to standing up and leaning forward.

This rider is making good use of her position in the air to balance a 'forward jump'. She is making good preparation to gain control on the landing stride.

This young horse is at his first show. The rider is very concerned that he remains in balance and confident throughout the jump. Note the look of pure innocence in the horse's expression.

Once you are in the correct position your muscles should be strong to assist in retaining your correct position but, at the same time, they should not be tense. It is not desirable for your muscles to be tight and hard. To ride with your muscles tight all the time will make you and your horse tense and stiff and will seriously decrease your enjoyment of riding and your horse's enjoyment of you! There should be no tightness in your back or shoulders. When sitting into the saddle in canter or sitting trot it is important to allow your hips to open and close with the movement of the horse – this needs a supple and relaxed body. If your position in the saddle is strong yet soft you will enable your horse to move and rise underneath you, so that he is free to use his shoulders and he is not thrown off balance by changes in your weight. A strong yet soft position will give your horse the freedom to perform well and you the confidence to ride well. Position is everything!

Basic Work on the Flat

THERE ARE TWO VERY IMPORTANT THINGS every rider should know. How does the horse work mechanically and how does he think? A horse is not a big person in a fur coat, or a cuddly toy; he is a horse. This means he is a reactionary creature, not a cunning predator who can reason and plan his way through life. The horse is, therefore, very easily distracted out of necessity; if he were dull-witted and not alert then in the wild he would become prey to predators. He must have lightning-quick reactions to stay alive. If we remember this very important point, then we can speed up our reactions and not be so easily taken off guard by something the horse may do.

Working your horse on the flat is an essential part of his education and will help you to keep him fit and healthy and prolong his jumping career. As a rider you need to understand the principles of how to work your horse at his most efficient, in other words, you need to master the basic techniques of riding your horse forward in a straight line with his body straight. This means that his hind legs should follow in the track of his forelegs and his hips should be in line with

International team rider and
*Head of Training for British
Show Jumping.*

DI LAMPARD

" I still have help with my riding. When I am riding on the flat, let alone jumping, I can only feel what my horse is doing. I need someone on the ground to see what the horse is doing and, by being told what he is doing I can put the two together to initiate improvement. "

his shoulders. We are not trying to control the horse; what we are trying to control is the impulsion we are producing. Controlled, forward impulsion is the very first rule; absolute straightness the second.

To perform at his best in the show jumping arena, your horse needs to be as supple and strong as his bodily structure will allow. Fundamentally, the horse is a grazing herd animal and his strongest instinct (along with feeding and reproduction) is that of flight – to go as fast as possible in a straight line – flexibility does not come into it, nor for that matter does jumping!

POINTS TO PONDER.... All the best riders do not own all the best horses, just the best trained ones.

The show jumping horse needs to be very flexible and very powerful.

Horses are not, therefore, inherently supple creatures and the supplest horse in the world will never be as flexible through the body as the most inflexible cat. However, by regular schooling on the flat, you can vastly improve your horse's suppleness.

Flatwork for show jumpers

The idea held by many young show jumping riders a few years ago, was that working a horse on the flat was boring and that they just wanted to get on with the jumping. This is now thankfully a thing of the past. Through great initiatives from the governing bodies of equestrian sport (particularly British Showjumping) and

Show jumping riders have come to learn the value of correct basic dressage. Here the horse is moving forward with a fairly low, long neck and good stretch along the top line.

Note the comparison between the dressage horse in medium trot and the show jumper in medium trot. The jumper is much stronger into the bridle whereas the dressage horse is much more 'up' and light. Neither is incorrect for their respective jobs.

UK Coaching's generic coaching programmes and certification, young riders are now aware that training is not boring and that a horse does not jump well without a strong foundation of correct work in basic 'show jumping' dressage. Work on the flat for the show jumper is very different from pure dressage. In show jumping the two primary aids are the legs and the hands with the rider sitting light on the horse while, in pure dressage, with the much longer stirrup leathers and the deeper seat, the seat becomes a primary aid. The seat and weight of the rider do have an influence in show jumping but this is mainly the influence of balance, rather than of direct control.

Defining objectives

So, let me define your immediate objectives in terms of control. Your ultimate aim when schooling a show jumper is to produce an athlete who:

- Can perform at his peak for a short period.
- Is instantly obedient to his rider's aids.
- Is (within the practical constraints of his physiology) 'infinitely adjustable' – see Adjusting the stride, later this chapter.
- Can alter the length and quickness of his stride at the merest indication from the rider.
- Has the strength and flexibility to leave all the fences standing in a faster time than all his rivals.

To do all this as calmly as possible as a consequence of:
- controlled forward impulsion
- even rhythm throughout all the gaits
- absolute straightness

- correct bend through every turn
- perfect balance.

Goal-setting

As mentioned in Chapter 1, goal-setting is important. Set yourself realistic, achievable goals but, even with short-term achievable goals, try not to set a time limit to realise them. Have a time in your head but if it doesn't happen in that timeframe then carry on, without deviating from the system. Some horses learn more quickly than others (and some horses learn some things quickly, but need more time to learn other things); some have better concentration; and some are more obedient than others (just like children). Above all, show patience and remember that an impatient rider will achieve nothing except frustration.

Also remember that no horse works at 100 per cent efficiency all the time; in truth, it is unlikely that most horses will ever perform at 100 per cent efficiency. Nonetheless, try to keep your horse's attention and feel him concentrating while he tries to get things right for you. Eventually you should feel that he is accepting the aids and working with you. *Listen* to your horse; he will tell you how to ride him. If he suddenly starts to rebel against what you are asking him to do, stop and ask yourself why. Is he becoming mentally or physically tired? Can he understand what you are asking him to do? Is he mentally and physically ready to do what you are asking him to do? Is what you are asking him to do hurting him – his muscles will ache just as much as yours would if he's asked to do something he hasn't done before.

So, let's get back to those basic tasks you need your horse to do: to go forward, stop, turn left and turn right. However, now we need to add in that the show jumper has to do each of these tasks *the instant* he is told to do so. If your horse starts to turn even one stride after you asked him to do so, he will miss the next fence altogether; even worse, you may panic and pull him off balance.

Moving off the leg

The first thing we need to teach the horse is that, when we close our legs on his sides, he must move forwards. Ask your horse to walk on by squeezing with your legs – has he moved? If not then, to connect with your horse's brain, you have to use your knowledge of his flight instinct to make him move forward. Ask him to walk on using your legs again, just as lightly, but this time back the leg aid up with a sharp smack with the schooling (long) whip at the same time. This time he will jump forward – allow him to and be careful to move with him and not to catch his mouth with the bit. This does not sound very pleasant but you should only ever need to do it once or twice before your horse learns to move instantly off your leg. The idea is that eventually you are able to use less, rather than more leg, to get a correct response from your horse. It is kinder that the horse learns obedience right from the beginning of his career than having to be retrained at a later date.

Here, a word about the 'spur school of thought', which dictates that you should wear spurs at all times and that, if a squeeze with the legs does not produce a response, then the spurs should be used to move the horse forward. In my experience very few novice riders are skilled enough to notice the subtle difference between riding with an 'inactive spur' and knowing exactly when they used the spur. Unstable legs with spurs can cause some very unhappy results. It is amazing how many times I have removed a rider's spurs on a supposedly 'hot' horse and that horse has almost immediately settled down. For this reason I prefer to see riders using the long schooling whip to back up the leg aids, until the leg position is firmly established. The spur should in fact, refine the aid, not make it.

And stopping

Now that you have your horse moving forward, you have to be able to stop him. Unlike pure dressage trainers, I believe that you should be able to stop your horse with the bit and reins alone, rather than combined with your seat, but your seat or position must be stable enough to allow you to give clear and succinct aids.

It is important in the arena that your horse can respond quickly to any change of contact on the rein, but again this only comes with training. However, the show jumping horse is naturally stronger than the average hack so your normal contact needs to be quite clearly defined and may, at times, be quite strong. It is quite acceptable to have a reasonably strong contact with your horse's mouth, so long as you can still maintain softness through the arms and elbows and ask him to slow down or speed up without him becoming resistant and unaccepting. If a small amount of increased pressure is not enough to stop your horse, then a more assertive hold needs to be taken until he comes to a halt or decreases his speed, as you have asked. But we must understand that, in riding terms, the greatest reward for the horse is a release of pressure, so the instant the horse accepts the aid we can, and must, relax the pressure.

Mechanically, your lower arms are extensions of the reins so they must act as shock-absorbers between your body and the horse's mouth. Imagine that your reins end at your elbows and not your hands. In this way it will be easier for you to picture your arms as a natural extension of the reins. If your elbows are too floppy this will create an uneven contact between the hands and the bit, leading to irregular pressure on the horse's mouth. This pressure would eventually cause your horse to become erratic and uneven in his gait as the discomfort increases. If your elbows are too stiff and clamped to your sides they will not be able to absorb any discrepancy between your hands and your horse's mouth. Your arms need to be elastic in order to absorb the movement between your body and the reins, as it is important that your hands remain still in relation to the *horse's head*, not still in relation to your *own body*, so that the contact between hands and bit remains constant.

The half-halt

The only tool that we have to teach the horse obedience to the rein aids is the transition. We have to develop the *half-halt* transition so that it becomes a natural indicator to the horse, that the rider is about to ask for a change of speed, gait, tempo or direction.

The expression half-halt is the way in which, in the equestrian vocabulary, we describe how we contain the horse's energy, prior to a change. What we are actually trying to do is condense the horse's stride for a brief moment and, in that moment, the horse has to engage his hocks, bring his forehand up and become more compact through collected energy.

Perfecting the half-halt so that it becomes a really effective aid takes many hours of patient work. We are looking for acceptance, not submission. In order that the half-halt is effective you have to have an instantaneous response to the leg and rein aids. To teach your horse to half-halt you must first teach him to halt. The halt does not have to be square, or the outline round, as it does in pure dressage, but it does have to happen when you ask for it. Make as many walk-to-halt/halt-to-walk transitions as it takes for your horse to learn that he must do each transition as soon as you ask him to, before progressing to trot-to-halt/halt-to-trot and canter-to-halt/halt-to-canter transitions. Remember that, on every occasion, the horse should respond briskly to your aids.

Once your horse can perform these transitions well, return to walk-to-halt transitions and reduce the amount of time you ask for the halt progressively, until the halt occurs for just a fraction of a second before you send him forwards again. Now, repeat the exercise in trot and canter. Each time you ask for the halt, your horse should feel, for a moment, like a coiled spring waiting to be let free – if he does, then you have perfected the half-halt. As you try to progress you will probably find that your horse has a seemingly endless repertoire of evasions; whether he twists his head, puts his tongue over the bit (this is less likely to happen if the bitting arrangement is satisfactory), crosses his jaw, throws his head up or down, your reaction must be the same. Do not lose your temper and continue to use the correct aids. Eventually he will hit on the idea that it is easier to do as he is told than to evade. It may take you several months to develop a consistently satisfactory half-halt but now you have the foundation for success.

To emphasise the point made earlier – the greatest reward for the ridden horse is the release of pressure, and horses very quickly come to realise that they can release the pressure themselves through acceptance of the aids.

Adjusting the stride

It is important that the show jumping horse becomes what I term *'infinitely adjustable'*. By this I mean that, in an instantaneous response to the aids, he should be able to make any adjustment to his speed and stride length that is within his physical capacity. To attain this adjustability you need to use your leg and rein aids and the half-halts, as I have described. Practise increasing and decreasing the tempo for short periods of five or six strides in trot and canter, making sure that the horse does not get away from you.

Start by quickening the stride rather than lengthening it, so that you have a feeling of going up-tempo, rather than becoming long and flat. Now try the same thing, only this time lengthen and shorten the stride; again do not lose control as then a fight will ensue while you try to regain it. Practise between two markers and see how many variations of stride pattern you can make, lengthening and shortening, quickening and slowing down. Eventually you will have a large number of variations within your horse's gait.

Lengthening and shortening the stride needs to be *through* the rein not *away from* the rein. In other words, when you ask the horse to lengthen, it is away from the leg whilst you are maintaining the contact; as opposed to using your leg aids, leaning forward and relinquishing the rein contact. The same rule applies to shortening the stride; the leg needs to be firm in support of the energy going forward, as opposed to the rider simply pulling on the rein. Think of shortening the stride by riding forward into a resisting hand.

Turning

Now that you can start and stop your horse and can lengthen, shorten, increase or decrease the tempo of his stride, you have to be able to turn him when you want to. It is easy to pull on one rein or the other and if you do so eventually your horse will turn, but it may not be at the time, in the manner or in the direction that you want him to, and good turns are a foundation of good jumping. So you have to be certain when you work your horse on the flat that he turns precisely where and how you want him to. This is up to you: you have to start thinking about the turn way ahead of where you want to execute it and you need to begin creating the bend as much as 5m (16ft 4in) before the turn actually begins. If your horse is flexible and is flexing in the direction of the turn, he will automatically bend more easily.

In the perfect turn each hand and each leg has a specific job. The outside rein is the most important because it is this rein that controls the horse. On the turn or circle the horse is naturally inclined to fall out toward the outside. If we adapt this instinct we can develop and train him to go to the outside rein in better balance and, when he is comfortable working into the outside hand, we will achieve more

control of his energy. By using your inside leg to push your horse's inside hind leg towards the outside rein, you can create a situation in which the control of your horse is very definitely in your outside rein. The inside rein can create the bend in the horse's body corresponding to the arc of the circle. The outside leg is used to prevent the horse from falling out of that arc.

An example of power in control through the turn.

The most common rider fault, when making a turn, is to pull on the inside rein and drop the outside rein – the result of which is that the horse falls out through the outside shoulder. A good reminder is to imagine the horse turning slightly *against* the outside rein.

Once you begin to turn your horse on to a circle you will begin to feel how balanced or, more likely, unbalanced he is. A young horse learns to balance himself naturally, but once in training, he needs to re-learn to balance, carrying his rider. Just like us, horses are right or left-handed and will, therefore, find it easier to perform in one direction than the other. It is your job to teach your horse to feel equally balanced on either rein.

If your horse feels unbalanced while walking or trotting on a circle he will either fall in (that is, he leans to the inside, putting too much weight on his inside shoulder and allowing his hindquarters to come off the true bend), or he will *fall out* (that is, he allows his outside shoulder – or whole body – to come off the correct bend towards the outside).

Bending is more than just having the skill to turn or make the horse look in the

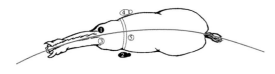

The aids for a correct bend.

• **The outside rein (1) and the inside leg (2).** The outside rein controls the horse's rhythm gait and speed and limits the amount of bend. It also affects his balance and carriage. The inside leg is the driving aid. By nudging the horse's side with the inside leg (using a momentary increase in pressure, not a flap) the horse is encouraged to bend around it. Once the horse has responded to the nudge by bending correctly, stop giving the aid and allow the inside leg to remain firmly against the horse's side, encouraging him to continue to bend around the leg.

• **The inside rein (3) and the outside leg (4).** The inside rein supports the bending aid of the inside leg. The inside rein should not be pulled back – this will cause too much bend in the neck or a tilting of the horse's head. The outside leg prevents the quarters from swinging out. It is positioned 10–12cm (approx. 4–5in) behind the girth. During sideways movements the outside leg may be used as a driving leg to promote forward, impulsive movement.

• **The rider's weight.** When asking for bend the inside hip **(5)** should carry fractionally more weight.

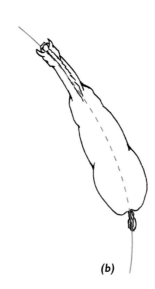

(a)   (b)   (c)

Straightness and bending.

*A truly straight horse **(a)** is able to bend his body equally to the left **(b)** and the right **(c)**.*

right direction. It is the fundamental and basic tool to make all of the interconnecting parts of the horse more efficient. Every time you bend a horse in one direction you are stretching the opposite side of him and developing the flexibility which enables the jumping horse to operate over wide obstacles. It also enables the horse to shorten with the right degree of impulsion and to maintain perfect balance. It is important to remember that flexion is possible without bend but bend is not possible without flexion.

Often the side of the horse that bends more easily to the inside can be the more difficult side. This is the side that the horse finds more difficult to stretch so he 'curls up' around the inside. Horses who have this habit must be encouraged initially to be straight on straight lines and then to develop equal flexibility on both sides.

Common bending problems.

(a)

(a) The horse tilts his head **(1)**, either to the outside – or more commonly – to the inside. Caused by pulling on the rein. Solution: decrease pressure on the pulling hand, use both legs to drive horse forward and straight; head will return to correct position **(2)**.

(b)

(b) The horse avoids bending his body by swinging his quarters out. Solution: lighten the inside rein, use outside leg and outside rein to prevent quarters from swinging out; strengthen inside leg to encourage horse to wrap around it.

(c)

(c) the horse avoids bending his body by letting his outside shoulder bulge outwards. Solution: use outside rein to prevent outward drift and lighten contact on the inside rein; ask the horse to move onto a straight line so that you can straighten his shoulder and neck before asking for bend again.

(d)

(d) The horse avoids bending his body by excessively bending his neck. Solution: increase pressure on the outside, controlling rein, and increase pressure on the inside, controlling leg; do not 'let go' of the inside, supporting rein. Frequent changes of direction will reduce the likelihood of the horse learning to avoid the bend.

Producing controlled impulsion

There is a world of difference between a horse who is slopping around anyhow and a horse who is moving and thinking forward. Your horse should feel full of impulsion and bounce, whether he is walking, trotting or cantering. To obtain this feeling it is necessary to contain your horse between rein and leg aids. By keeping your legs firmly on his sides and by controlling excessive forward movement with your reins, your horse should begin to feel athletic with a spring in his step. I call the slopping around with no obvious goal the *'wandering about aimlessly club'*; unfortunately it has many members!

To avoid becoming a member of the aforementioned club, think of a ball; the more air or pressure that is used to inflate the ball, the higher it will bounce and yet all that pressure is kept contained in the ball by its covering. If there is a hole in the ball, the energy will escape and the ball will become flat, much as your horse will if you cannot contain him between rein and leg. As a rider you must learn to put pressure on your horse until he is bouncing.

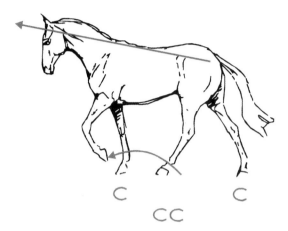

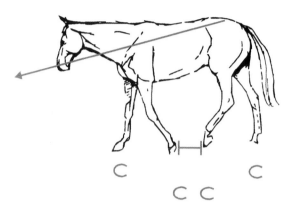

An active walk. *The horse is in a 'uphill' shape; his hindquarters are engaged and pushing his hind leg forwards powerfully. He is, therefore, 'tracking up' – his hind hoof is placed in front of the track left by the front hoof.*

A lazy walk. *The horse is in a 'downhill' shape; he is not engaging his hindquarters, therefore he is not 'tracking up'.*

A colourful picture I use to describe this kinetic energy we need to develop is the simple act of blowing up a balloon. The more the balloon expands, the more energy is contained. Then what happens if you prick the balloon with a pin? It explodes. On the other hand, what happens if you blow up your balloon and, when it is full, you simply let go? Well then, all the energy just fizzles out. So pump up your horse and let the jump be the pin and *wham*, you get a big explosion over the fence.

A strong 'uphill' canter.

In this picture the rider has tremendous concentration on where he intends to go.

An interesting view of the intense pressure the horse puts on his pastern joints and the strength of the hind leg and the forearm.

In general, grass-roots riders will be seen trying to chase their horses along, in an effort to make them go faster, when in fact they are really only succeeding in making them go flat i.e. letting go of the balloon. The best way to improve your horse's forwardness is to keep practising the exercises we have discussed for making your horse more responsive. Changes of tempo and length of stride will increase your horse's awareness of your aids, and half-halts will help to collect him, making his gaits rounder and stronger.

The importance of all of this work is that it will enable you to:

- Ride your horse at a correct speed to jump the fence.
- Stay in balance at that speed.
- Maintain that speed in a rhythm.
- Develop enough power to jump the fence.

Remember to be careful and not to join the 'wandering around aimlessly club', not a lot, if any of its members, are successful show jumping riders!

POINTS TO PONDER...

The harder you work the luckier you will get.

More Advanced Work on the Flat

RIDERS WHO DO NOT RECOGNISE that their horse is ready to move from one stage in his development to another tend to make their horses stiffer and weaker, inverted and set in the jaw, so once your horse is moving forward in a straight and energetic way, you can begin to increase his flexibility by introducing him to lateral work. I like my horses to be able to leg-yield and to perform shoulder-in and travers (haunches-in). If this all sounds too technical, it's not, so read on.

Before you get into this part of the chapter we need to go through some of the jargon used in lateral work. For argument's sake we will assume that you are working in an enclosed arena with two long sides, two short sides and, therefore, four corners. In order that you can follow the exercises easily we will also assume

A short, active and elevated trot; flatwork of this quality is a useful attribute for a show jumper.

Ireland's leading International rider and a consummate horseman.

SHANE BREEN

"Young riders or anyone aspiring to be a successful show jumper should never undervalue the importance of good flatwork based on sound dressage theories. Your horse should be as flexible and obedient as possible. A flexible body will give your horse a flexible mouth, and obedience will give your horse an accepting mind."

that your arena measures 40–60m on the 'long' side and 20m on the 'short' side, just as a dressage arena is laid out, with markers to guide you. Unless I talk about a circle at the centre of the arena (between B and E) you can assume that a circle commences at A or C.

When working on the 'outside track' you are working as near to the outside rails as is practically and safely possible. The 'inside track' technically, can be anywhere between the outside rails and the centre line of your arena but, more often than not, the term 'inside track' is used to describe an invisible line about 1–3m in from the 'outside track'. When you work your horse on the flat, try to work him on the inside track and down the centre line as often as you do on the outside track, so that he does not become dependent on the rails to stay straight. In fact, I try hard not to use the track against the wall or rail at all; it is a good discipline and makes me more aware of the *outside* of the horse as well as the *inside*.

Now for the technical bits! Horses are often described as working on two, three or four tracks. This alludes to where the horse places his feet. If he is working on two tracks, his hind feet will travel along the same line as his forefeet*; if he is working on three tracks, his near-fore will move on one line, his off-fore and near-hind will move on a second and his off-hind will move on a third. If he is working on four tracks, his near-fore will be moving on one line, his off-fore on a second, his near-hind on a third and his off-hind on a fourth – easily done unintentionally if your horse is excitable but much more difficult to achieve on purpose.

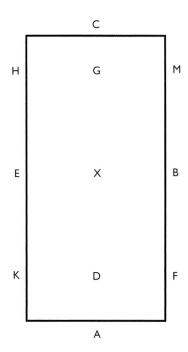

Standard 20 x 40m schooling area.

* But beware: although this definition is clearly true, the phrase 'two-track' work has been used traditionally (and very loosely) to refer to almost any form of lateral work, in which the horse is usually working on three or four tracks! The 'rationale' to this usage is that the hindquarters (as a unit) are not aligned behind the forehand.

The leg-yield

The leg-yield involves your horse going forwards and sideways at the same time, by crossing his fore and hind legs. Your horse's outside hind leg provides the power for the movement, stepping sideways first, as the inside leg then moves across in front of it. I use leg-yield a lot as I feel that any exercise that makes a horse cross his legs is beneficial. Why? Because all the time we ride a horse forward, asking him to work in a straight line, whether lengthening or shortening the stride, increasing or decreasing the tempo, we may be increasing his agility and balance, but it does little to improve his *flexibility*. So we come to one of life's big paradoxes, which is that a horse can't be truly straight until he is able to truly bend. In other words, for a horse to be able to move well in a straight line, he must have supple limbs. How do we achieve supple limbs? By asking the horse to bend! The Germans call it *'schwung'*: in English the nearest we can come to *'schwung'* is 'looseness, self-carriage, balance and forwardness' – roll those into one and you simply get 'swing through the body'.

We can begin to leg-yield on the circle by increasing the size of the circle by pushing the horse to the outside with the inside leg whilst maintaining the bend; this will start to prepare the horse for the leg-yield on the straight line. Then we can progress to using the centre line. Ride down the centre line keeping the horse's body straight but with a slight inside flexion (away from the direction of the

Below left: The horse's hind legs crossing in the leg-yield.

Below right: The horse's forelegs crossing in the leg-yield.

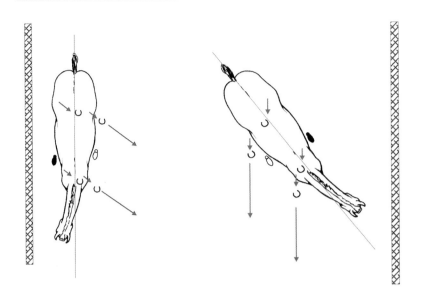

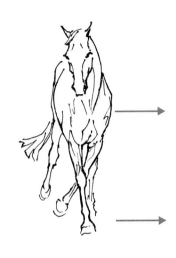

Leg-yield.
In leg-yielding, whether carried out across the diagonal (far left) or along the side of the arena (middle), the horse's body remains straight whilst his legs cross. His neck may be flexed slightly away from the movement. The horse moves away from the rider's active outside leg; the rider's less active inside leg should support the outside leg, controlling the horse's hindquarters.

intended movement). We can now start to push him toward the outside wall (either to the left or right as required) using the inside leg; this may have to be backed up with the long whip or the light touch of the spur to emphasise the clarity of the aid. Up until now the leg has only been understood as an aid to go forward and so we are likely to need to make clear with the half-halt aid that there is to be no increase in tempo.

As his training progresses, the sideways angle of your horse can be as steep or as shallow as you wish. As he becomes well established in lateral work he may, for example, be able to leg-yield from K to B, but initially you should aim to travel from K to M, (both these diagonals are, of course, steeper angles in a small arena than a large one) or from quarter marker to quarter marker. It is important that your horse's body remains pretty straight because if you allow him to bend excessively though the neck he will begin to fall out through the shoulders. A small amount of bend, away from the leg aid, is acceptable to begin with but your ultimate aim is to have the horse's spine straight and his legs crossing.

As with the shoulder-in (see below), once you have perfected the leg-yield at walk, you can progress to carrying it out at trot, but one of the most important points to remember with either movement, is that it is better to ride a small angle well with good control, balance and rhythm, than an acute angle badly.

The shoulder-in

I use the shoulder-in as the fundamental lateral exercise for the show jumper. The shoulder-in involves your horse keeping his hindquarters on the outside track, whilst his body bends evenly so that his inside hind leg follows the same (or a

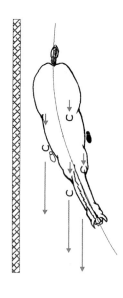

similar) track to his outside foreleg while his inside foreleg is on the inside track. It is not an exercise in which you are trying to gain points but rather an exercise in which you are trying to encourage your horse to move through his inside hind leg and through his shoulder, without losing his balance. One way of picturing the shoulder-in is to imagine that you are riding a 20m circle with a correct bend throughout your horse's body and that, as you come off that 20m circle on to the long side, you still maintain that correct, even bend, even though you are now travelling in a straight line, on three or four tracks depending on the stage in the horse's training and the angle of the shoulder-in.

The most important thing to remember before you start to ask for a shoulder-in is that your horse must be absolutely in balance on the circle, before you attempt to go straight, because whether he is working on three or four tracks, if he is running out through his outside shoulder, he is falling to the outside and not performing a shoulder-in. In other words, he is going sideways with a stiff, resistant spine rather than moving forwards with a supple, flexing spine. The essential part of this movement is that your horse's weight is carried by his inside hind leg and that he is pushing himself sideways through that hind leg, rather than the weight being on his outside shoulder, in which case he is dragging himself along on the forehand.

Preparation for the shoulder-in

The aids are pretty much uniform in all the exercises we do:

Shoulder-in.
In shoulder-in the horse's body becomes equally curved throughout its entire length. In this diagram the shoulder-in is being performed on three tracks. Remember that your active leg should be supported by your passive leg.

- Your inside leg is used to bring the inside hind leg of your horse underneath him to push him forward. It 'produces energy'.
- Your outside leg prevents his quarters from swinging out. It 'controls the energy'.
- Your inside rein is used to position your horse's shoulder off the outside track.
- Once your horse is in position, the inside rein becomes light, purely maintaining that position.
- The outside rein, which your horse is moving towards, controls his energy and power.

The angle of the shoulder-in should be dictated mainly by the stage of your horse's schooling; as he becomes more advanced and supple, the angle of shoulder-in can become more acute, progressing from three to four tracks. (Be mindful that trying for four tracks too early is likely to result in a form of leg-yield along the track, lacking the physical benefits of shoulder-in. Although leg-yielding has its values, it is a different exercise from shoulder-in and, in this context, it would simply be an error.) However, while it is always an error to ask for too *much* angle too soon, there is no harm in asking for a *lesser* angle than the horse can produce, as a preparatory exercise. A very slight amount of bend/angle is often called 'shoulder-fore' rather than shoulder-in. You should begin your shoulder-in at walk and, when this feels well established, you can progress to trot.

Travers

The travers or haunches-in is the most advanced lateral exercise that I will teach the show jumping horse. As with all lateral exercises, its purpose is to engage the horse's hindquarters and to increase his flexibility. Basically, travers is a half-pass with the horse's head on the outside track, bent in the direction of the movement, and the horse's quarters on the inside track. In this exercise it is the horse's outside leg moving across in front of the inside leg that provides the impulsion for the movement.

What you must avoid is blocking the action of one leg with the other. So, if you are trying to produce activity with the inside leg and to push the horse along the wall with the outside leg, you may find yourself in a situation where your inside leg, asking for impulsion, is blocking the action of the outside leg, asking for the bend. (Sometimes, the reverse may also be true, with the action of the leg asking for bend blocking the action of the leg asking for impulsion. In such a case, remember the axiom that, in lateral work, the bend/angle should never override the forward impulse.) Therefore your inside leg must produce enough power and activity as you come off the corner of the arena, to be able to just rest it against your horse's side as he moves into travers on the long side. The action of your outside leg is exaggerated; it is not just controlling your horse's quarters but manipulating them, bending the quarters inwards. The inside leg is still producing activity; the inside rein is still bending and the outside rein is still controlling.

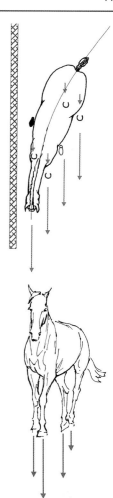

Travers.
In travers, as in shoulder-in, the horse's body becomes equally curved throughout its entire length. In this diagram the travers is being performed on three tracks. Remember that your active leg should be supported by your passive leg.

The rein-back

The rein-back is a very important exercise. Unlike the walk, which is four-beat, the rein-back is two-beat, more like a trot in reverse without a moment of suspension. It increases your horse's flexibility through his spine and hind leg joints, puts power into his hocks before he moves forwards and also demonstrates that he is fully submissive and obedient. When your horse is totally submissive to the rein-back he is much easier to control. Imagine, if you will, that when you ask

POINTS TO PONDER...

Nothing can pull against nothing, so don't pull – push.

your horse to rein-back, he lifts his head, crossing his jaw, hollows his back and will not move – or he goes sideways. Now multiply that feeling by one hundred and imagine you are approaching a fence while trying to ask your horse to slow down. Disconcerting, isn't it? If your horse is not submissive to all your rein and leg aids then this will begin to happen.

The rein-back is not a natural movement for the horse and, at first, he will find it quite difficult. In fact, it begins by being a trick and eventually evolves into a correct movement. To move backwards he must tilt his pelvis and raise his back – not easy – especially with the weight of a rider on his back. I teach my horses to rein-back in the stable at the long-reining stage before I get on them. If a young horse learns to go backwards from a voice command to begin with and then with the voice command backed up by the rein aid, it will make the job far easier when you get on top.

To teach your horse to rein-back when ridden, it is easier if you have an assistant on the ground to help you. First, position your legs slightly behind the girth, to prevent your horse from moving sideways, and then ride him quietly forwards with your legs, into an unyielding rein contact. As your horse submits he finds he can't move forwards, because your hands prevent that and he can't move sideways because your legs prevent that, so he moves backwards to the leg aid. As you ask your horse to move back your assistant can gently tap the horse's shins with a dressage whip while you back up the aids with a verbal command: 'Back'. Continue practising the exercise until your horse is moving backwards confidently in a straight line and then attempt the rein-back on your own. Never force the movement and only ever ask for four or five steps of rein-back at a time as continually repeating the movement will put strain on your horse's joints.

Once you have perfected the rein-back you can begin to use it as a tool to improve your horse's gaits. Teach your horse to walk, trot and canter immediately from the rein-back and also teach him to walk forwards a couple of strides, then rein-back, then trot forwards for five strides, then rein-back, walk forwards three strides then into rein-back, etc. This 'rocking' not only helps your horse to engage his hocks but also sharpens his mind and teaches him not to anticipate. A great part of your job as a show jumper is to get your horse's weight on to his hind legs and off his forelegs so that he is light in front and active behind. After all, our ultimate aim is to get one stride right – the take-off stride. If your horse has all his power in his hind legs and his front end is light he can push himself over the fence.

The canter

The canter consists of a series of bounds and is the gait from which show jumping horses jump. Therefore it is the gait that you have to perfect if you want to show jump well – or at all. When cantering *true*, your horse should canter in a three-time beat, with the outside hind leg striking off first (first beat), then the inside hind leg and outside foreleg move together (second beat) and the inside fore, the leading leg, following (third beat), before a moment of suspension. You should not be able to hear four hoof-beats during the canter – this is a sign of lack of impulsion and means that the hind legs are not engaged but are running to keep up!

In the counter-canter or false canter the horse canters with the right lead, on a left-hand circle and with a left lead, on a right-hand circle. I would only use the counter-canter to help a horse who is particularly stiff on one rein or the other and to strengthen the canter generally. The important thing to remember, if you do use the counter-canter, is to control your horse's quarters because if you allow his quarters to swing in he will become disunited; which means that the leading foreleg is on the opposite side to the leading hind leg. This is not only very uncomfortable for the rider but is also unbalancing for the horse – and he would not be able to make a good jump from a disunited canter.

To show jump well the horse must be well trained, be in balance, be 'infinitely adjustable' and must have a good canter. The action of jumping is purely an exaggerated canter stride, therefore, if your horse's canter is powerful and in balance, so will his jump be.

A horse who is well trained is 'infinitely adjustable' and such a horse has to be in complete balance or self-carriage whilst maintaining power without your help. He has to maintain this self-carriage each time you ask him to increase or decrease his length or speed of stride so that he can remain in balance.

Exercises to improve the canter

One of the exercises I do to improve the canter is to construct a 20m square on the ground using poles. At the four corners I place four cones about 5m in. Using such a set-up, start by trotting your horse between the poles and the cones and, when he feels confident at trot, progress to canter. When he is trotting and cantering around the square in good balance, you can reduce the square to 15m and bring the cones closer to the corners. At each corner your horse has to take a powerful stride with his inside hind leg to propel himself around the bend and, as the square becomes smaller and the angle of the corner more acute, his weight is taken completely by that leg.

Another exercise to improve the canter uses the long side of the arena. Canter your horse along the long side and then, as you reach the corner, turn him on a 10m half-circle and canter down the centre line. As you reach the end of the arena, turn again on a 10m half-circle to the outside track. Each time you have completed the turn keep the canter straight on the long side. As your horse's canter and balance improves you can reduce the half-circle to 8m.

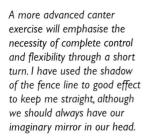

A clear illustration of the canter square exercise. The horse needs to be kept on the outside aids and still remain very active. Trot around the cones to begin with and graduate to canter as the balance improves.

Spiralling in from a 20m circle down to a 10m circle and out again to a 20m circle is also an excellent canter exercise. Again, you can eventually reduce the inward spiral to an 8m circle as your horse's canter improves.

An exercise which is useful to prevent your horse from falling in on his corners is to canter him along the short side of the arena, halt and turn into the wall and canter back along the short side. Concentrate on creating a powerful halt–canter transition.

A trotting exercise to improve your horse's bend and balance (which will pay dividends in the canter work) is to trot along the long side and, at the corner of the arena, begin a 10m circle but, as you reach the centre line, having completed a half-circle, move diagonally back to the outside track, trotting back to the next corner to repeat the exercise. Concentrate on creating correct bends and straightness.

A more advanced canter exercise will emphasise the necessity of complete control and flexibility through a short turn. I have used the shadow of the fence line to good effect to keep me straight, although we should always have our imaginary mirror in our head.

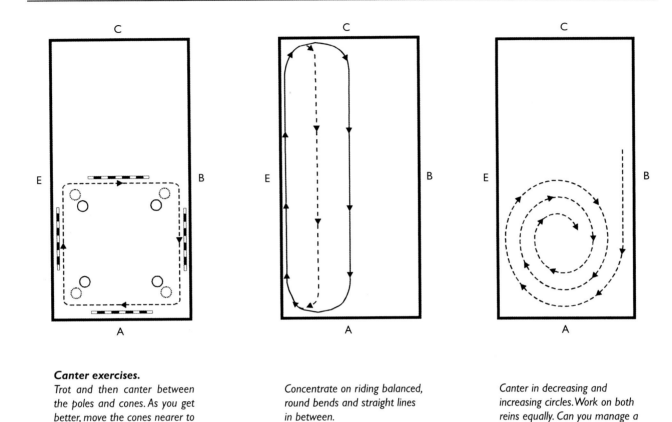

Canter exercises.
Trot and then canter between the poles and cones. As you get better, move the cones nearer to the corners.

Concentrate on riding balanced, round bends and straight lines in between.

Canter in decreasing and increasing circles. Work on both reins equally. Can you manage a 8m circle?

The flying change

All show jumpers need to be able to do flying changes. The flying change required for show jumping is a more utilitarian, forward-going and less collected one than the change required in a dressage test. It is a necessity during the show jumping round that the horse can change direction fluidly. You don't have time in the arena to stop, change leg and start again, so it is important that the horse is on the correct lead going around the corner toward the fence, to maintain all the other qualities of the canter that we have discussed.

I like to teach my horses the flying change as part of their formative training, as they are learning to canter on a circle. Some people will raise their eyebrows and pronounce that you need to have an established, balanced canter before you attempt to teach the flying change, but I believe that if you ask horses to do 'new tricks' when they are innocent and offering to do things for you, then the job becomes more a game and less of a drama. A horse cantering loose in the school or field will often perform a flying change quite naturally so we are only trying to transform a natural movement into something we can instigate at a given time with a given sign.

POINTS TO PONDER...
Horses generally do as they are told, so tell them to do the right things.

To prepare for a flying change, make sure that your horse is in balance and has enough impulsion in his hind legs to make the jump from one hind leg to the other. The *hind leg* are the operative words because if the horse changes legs behind, he will invariably change in front, but if he changes in front it does not necessarily follow that he will also change behind. To obtain the change you should try to physically change your horse's bend and physically push the quarters over.

For example, if you have been on a right-hand circle with a right-hand lead and have your horse's quarters on a right-hand bend then, as you ride across the diagonal from one quarter marker to the other, you move your horse on to the left bend with his quarters moving to the left and, as you ask the quarters to move across and change their bend, so the hind legs should automatically change their lead, following through with a change of the forelegs. Effectively you have put your horse on to the left hind leg; while this is not the leg that *initiates* the left canter stride it is now the inside hind leg which will support the horse on the bend, and thus the horse will be supporting himself through the left corner.

Remember your basics and what each hand and leg is meant to do. As you ask for the change, your inside supporting hand becomes your outside controlling hand and your outside controlling leg becomes the inside driving leg but, as you change the bend, you must offer your horse some support with the outside rein so that he does not fall on to the forehand. As you change your aids, you are physically changing the bend and pushing the quarters slightly towards the inside, to make him move from one hind leg to the other.

Initially, ride your horse across the diagonal, ask him to perform a flying change and see what he offers. If he performs a change without any problem, breathe a sigh of relief and say: 'Thank goodness for that!' If he does not then you have to think about other methods of teaching him this movement. The important thing is that you must be able to maintain balance throughout the change. It is not a case of throwing your horse off the balance of one shoulder and then throwing him on to the other and hoping that he changes – he may well – but he will almost certainly change legs in front and not behind. This is the most common fault seen in the jumping arena.

The fault some riders make is to aim their horses towards a wall when asking for a flying change. This makes the horse very defensive and he will not change legs so freely, as he backs off the wall and throws his weight on to the shoulder. It is not in fact important where you ask for the change of leg – you can ask for the change of lead on the diagonal or you can make a canter circle and ask for it as you change direction, on to the opposite circle, as in a figure of eight; or you can change from counter-canter to true canter on a straight line. It is better that you vary the place of asking for the change so that your horse learns to listen to the aids, rather than looking to change automatically at a certain point.

Show jumping horses develop an instinct for changing legs on the corner

anyway, as they have to do it so often, and you can use this anticipation to help perform the exercise. Most young horses are quite willing to perform a flying change naturally and quickly learn to change to order, when given the correct aids. A few horses genuinely do find it physically difficult to change legs in canter and for these horses we have to try to teach the flying change and to do that, we certainly do need to have a better canter. (Some horses may find it harder to change from one particular lead to the other, perhaps because they have residual stiffness/one-sidedness – in which case further attention to overall suppleness can alleviate the problem.)

To teach your horse the flying change, use a small pole, raised about 15cm (6in)

Here is a good example of how the running rein can help with the flying change to stop the horse running through the bridle.

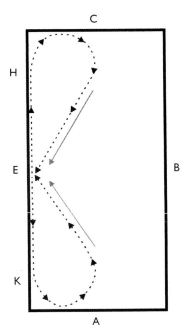

Exercise to improve bend and balance. At trot, maintain the bend you have created through the half-circle until you reach the wall at H and K.

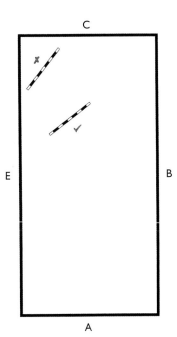

Teaching the flying change. Place a cavalletto or low pole in the centre of the arena and change legs as the horse comes off the ground.

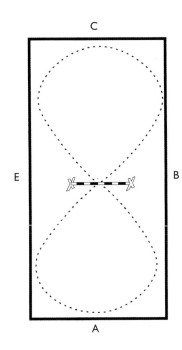

Using poles to teach the flying change (see text). Do not put the poles too near to the wall – it makes the horse back off.

off the ground, in the middle of your arena, as the centre of a figure of eight, and change legs as the horse comes off the ground. In order to do this you have to have good balance and timing. You need to keep your horse in balance all the way to the pole and, as he comes off the ground, you need to change the bend and shift your weight slightly so that your inside leg becomes the outside leg, etc. It is important to use your eye and sense of rhythm and an open rein rather than a pulling hand. Use the pole to enable your horse to get into the habit of changing legs as he changes direction. Then you can put the pole near the end of the diagonal line, coming towards the corner, so that as you come across the pole he changes leg on to the new lead. When you feel your horse responding confidently to your aids you can lower the pole and then take it away altogether.

Finding a Good Distance for Take-Off

WHEN COACHING JUMPING RIDERS the question that I get asked most frequently is: 'What is "seeing a stride", or "finding a good distance"?' My answer is: 'The gift of always knowing exactly at which spot the horse should take off to jump cleanly with minimum effort, and having the fundamental ability to alter the horse's approach, to enable the horse to arrive at that correct take-off point.'

Riders tend to overlook the facts that horses are neither blind nor stupid. They can see where they are going and see what is front of them; their eyes will tell their brain and their brain will tell their body how to react and what they need to do – it's called *mind/body co-ordination*. Humans all have this facility too, so let's use it to our best advantage. The horse has an inbuilt instinct for survival, combined with a very long memory. In his natural state, without a rider on his back to alter his balance and rhythm, a horse will instinctively set himself up for a fence and will take off at the correct place time and time again. If a good rider gets on the horse and rides him in rhythm and balance and at the correct speed to a fence, enabling the horse to take off from the correct spot every single time, it will not be very long before the horse starts to remember where that spot is and begins to aim for it himself, provided of course, that he is not interfered with.

Remember too, that the horse's ability to judge distances is a great deal more accurate than our own and that his innate instinct is much sharper than ours, so his brain is actually working more quickly than his rider's. However, the horse is a also prey animal and his instinct, when faced with danger, is to flee. So, when the horse gets into a situation that he finds difficult or threatening, such as an incorrect or panicky approach to a jump, he will instinctively panic himself. This is likely to produce the result we all fear – the horse will come to an abrupt halt in front of the fence, a prelude to turning around and running away. Occasionally he will crash straight through the jump in blind panic. Alternatively, he may jump too high in

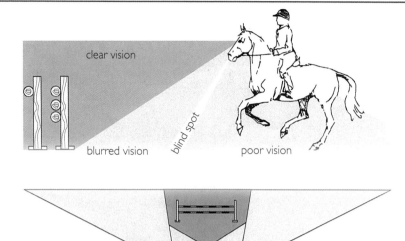

As the horse approaches the fence with his head held in a natural, forward-looking position, he can see very little of what is on either side of him.

Within a stride of the fence:

1. With the horse's head held high, this area is blurred; if the horse lowered his head, this area could become clearer to him.
2. Area of clear, sharp focus.
3. Area of good, long-distance vision.
4. Area of poor vision; the horse can only register moving objects unless he turns his head to one side or the other.

an attempt to protect himself, but doing so will frighten him and he will be more inclined to stop next time.

Once we have accepted these points – most positively the fact that the horse can jump correctly by himself, then we are ready to add ourselves to the equation. Problems start to occur when riders are not consistent. Some riders will approach the same fence 20 times and never take off from the same spot twice. This is when the horse starts to get confused and the more confused he becomes, the more his confidence ebbs away, leading to a rapid decline in his desire to jump. First he becomes a little stressed because he doesn't know where he is going to be asked to take off from, and then he becomes tense, and this tension and stress lead to further confusion. At this point the horse starts to hesitate, then the more he hesitates, the more mistakes he makes and a downward spiral begins, usually ending up with a horse who refuses to jump at all.

The mistake that has been made by so many trainers in the past is that they have tried to standardise the correct take-off point by giving a set formula such as: 'The take-off point for a 1.25m (4ft 2in) fence is exactly that same distance away from the fence'. Unfortunately, no two horses are alike and what may be the correct take-off point for one may be way off the mark for another. If your horse is slow to fold up his forelegs but is careful behind, his ideal take-off point is going to be further away from the fence than a horse who is quick in front but who can be lazy with his hind legs. So we are not trying to get to a *take-off* spot but to arrive in good shape in the *take-off* zone. The take-off zone can be 0.9m (3ft) in width; that is to say the furthest extremities of the zone can be 0.9m (3ft apart) and these extremities may be 0.3m (1ft) either side of the ideal spot. The more important points are: can the horse take you to the fence with the canter you have produced and, can he jump correctly from that canter?

The fundamental rule to remember, when you are riding to a fence, is this:

POINTS TO PONDER....

The horse's reaction will be very quick and he won't slow down for you, so speed up!

maintain the correct speed and tempo to jump the particular fence you are coming to in balance and rhythm. This is a rule that comes up time and time again throughout this book because it is the one important factor that remains constant. There are a very few gifted riders who have the innate ability to judge distances absolutely and consistently but, for the majority, it is a case of training hard to learn to keep the stride constant and not continually changing the tempo. My firm belief is that if you ride to the fence consistently and often, your eye will, in time, train itself. It is all about teaching the horse self-reliance through consistency, not riding in deep *(too close)* to force the horse to try harder and harder. The modern show jumping horse will not tolerate being threatened in this way; he is too sensitive and careful.

The terrain is also very important. If you are jumping downhill your horse will naturally come to his fence on a slightly longer, flatter stride, unless you keep him collected between your legs and your hands and again, keep the stride constant. As he is more able to cover the ground when jumping downhill, the point at which your horse will take off will be slightly further away than if you are on the flat, so the need to keep in balance is even more important. When jumping uphill it is important to keep up the strength and impulsion of the canter so that your horse doesn't run out of steam before he reaches the jump. The take-off point, when jumping uphill, will be closer to the fence than when jumping on the flat, so it will be necessary to maintain a more powerful, shorter stride.

Heavy going underfoot also influences where your horse takes off from – heavy going can add 10cm (4in) to the total height of the fence. Your horse needs to take off nearer to the fence to enable him to pull out of the mud but he needs to have enough power and marginally more speed, to stay within his comfort zone.

From more advanced riders the question I am most frequently asked is: 'How can I improve my ability to see a stride?' The short answer is: 'It's not easy.' (And, can I add, it is not always that important!) The truth is that you simply don't need to over small fences. Every trainer in the world has tried a hundred different ways to explain 'how to see a stride' but no one has come up with the magic formula yet. Perhaps, rather cynically, my favourite reply to the question is: 'Everyone can see a stride…but more often than not, it's a bad one.' If you follow the methods described below then, in time, your eye will naturally develop and your ability to judge distance will improve.

The first thing you have to have to decide when approaching the fence is the speed or tempo at which you are to travel. In deciding the speed of the approach it is necessary to include the horse's nature in the equation. To ask a naturally fast and fizzy horse to go slowly is likely to make him pent up and upset. He will learn to go against the rider, begin to hollow and will ultimately become uncontrollable. You have to allow him to move forwards – but under control. Having found the tempo at which the horse is happy to be ridden, you then have to discipline yourself to maintain that tempo and to ride the horse at his fences in that tempo.

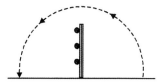

On the flat. The trajectory you make over the fence is an even semi-circle.

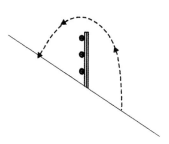

Jumping uphill. You will need a shorter, steeper trajectory to clear the fence. Your take-off point will have to be closer to the fence than if it were on the flat.

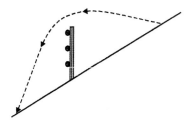

Jumping downhill. You will need a longer, flatter trajectory to clear the fence. Your take-off point will have to be further away from the fence than if it were on the flat.

It is important to maintain that same speed and rhythm throughout the approach. You also have to understand that you may have to alter the tempo for the approach to different fences. A skinny foot stile will, for example, require a slower, more cautious approach than a big, wide oxer, which will need a bolder approach.

At the beginning you have to convince yourself that the jump is the least important part of the equation, that it is the stride pattern and the tempo, which are all-important. I tell my riders to forget about the fence altogether so they are concentrating entirely on a rhythmic canter, in other words on maintaining the tempo. The horse is then able to concentrate on looking forward and is focusing his attention forward rather than thinking backwards, about what the rider is going to do or not do, in order to make a mess of jumping the approaching fence.

If the horse is worried about what the rider on his back is going to do next then he is not going to be focused on the fence ahead but, if you can ignore the poles and can just set the stride pattern up, then he is not going to be thinking about you but about the fence ahead. It is incredibly difficult not to think about the approaching jump, so it is very important that you keep the fences small until you feel totally confident riding to the fence without worrying about whether or not you can see a stride.

Improving your judgement of distance

The greatest tool for improving your judgement of distance is a balanced, rhythmic canter that has controlled impulsion. Without a good canter it is impossible to achieve a good jump. Exercises to improve the canter are mentioned elsewhere, but a good one to help you start improving your ability to keep a good canter, on the approach to and in between fences, is to put two poles on the ground approximately five non-jumping strides (about 22m/72ft) apart. Set up your canter in another part of the school and get a good rhythm and correct tempo. Come off the corner and canter towards the poles with the sole purpose of maintaining that rhythm and tempo. Focus on a point beyond the poles and don't be tempted to look down at them as you cross them.

Don't worry if your horse leaps the poles wildly or gets six or even seven strides between them; just continue on your route, trying to keep the rhythm. Once your horse is cantering evenly through the poles on five strides, try to decrease the tempo so that he gets six or seven strides in between them. Although you are trying to shorten your horse's stride, try also to maintain impulsion in the canter but remember not to look down at the poles. You are trying to develop a feel for the correct canter and looking down will shift your focus. Next, increase the tempo so that he gets just four strides between the poles, but don't let the canter become flat.

Once you feel totally confident carrying out this exercise, without looking at the poles, you are ready to raise them a little, but be sensible, the main object of the

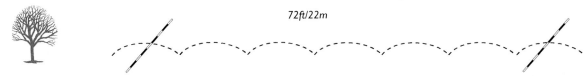

72ft/22m

Canter exercises between two poles. *Try to maintain five regular strides between the two poles. Remember to relax and look ahead at the tree, not down at the poles.*

72ft/22m

Now try to lengthen your horse's stride. Ask for four regular strides between the two poles.

72ft/22m

Try to shorten your horse's stride. Ask for six regular strides between the two poles.

exercise is to increase your confidence, not the size of the fences. By learning to alter your horse's canter stride you are increasing your chances of being able to reach the fence at the correct take-off point and you are giving yourself a greater range of options. If you repeat the exercise enough you will start to pick up from a long way back, not only how many strides in terms of numbers it will take to arrive at the fence, but whether or not the rhythm and tempo you have will bring you to the fence at the correct take-off point.

Canter poles will help your eye to develop naturally.

Canter poles placed in front of the fence will give the horse and rider confidence to ride forward in rhythm to the jump.

Using your eye to look forward on the approach, in the air and immediately on landing will make you more aware and sharpen your reaction time.

Another good exercise to help you develop your feel and judgement is to lay down seven or eight poles 3.0m (9ft 9in) apart and to canter over them. Again, remember not to look at the poles; just maintain your horse's rhythm. Eventually it will become instinctive and therefore easier. You are aiming for your horse to canter though this grid without altering his stride or tempo in any way. When you are confidently riding through the grid of poles you can put a small fence at the end of it, 3m (9ft 9in) from the final pole. This will teach you how it is possible to maintain a good canter at least seven or eight strides away from the fence and, eventually, on the whole approach from your initial turn.

Once you have developed the skill of being able to approach a fence without the need to look at it, by feeling the horse's stride working correctly underneath you, you will begin to feel more confident. You will be able to concentrate more and more on keeping your horse at the correct speed and rhythm and be satisfied that you are riding in balance. You will begin to know instinctively whether that point is a good or bad place from which to take off. If that point is a bad one, then you will have to make an adjustment. The adjustment that you make is crucial. You have two choices – to lengthen the stride or to shorten it – but you have just one opportunity to get it right. That one opportunity comes at the precise moment that you realise you are not going to meet the fence at the correct point. If you don't make that one, instantaneous, correction you will begin to panic and will either pull or push until you make a mess of things; either way your horse will lose balance and confidence.

The more you continue to ride at fences without worrying about them, the greater the distance will become from which you can be confident of arriving at them in good form, to jump them well. Top-class riders are able to tell from ten or twelve strides away from the fence, whether or not they are going to take off from the correct point for their horse. The very best will do this entirely naturally; however, many top riders are just very well trained and have attained this sense of judgement through practice. You cannot expect or hope to be as good as the very best, but hard work will help you to achieve a sense of balance, rhythm, tempo and judgement which you can continue to improve on throughout your show jumping career. Once again remember, in time your eye will train itself.

Getting from Fence to Fence – and Leaving Them Up

NOW WE CAN GO ON TO WHAT YOU HAVE TO DO to make a good jump. You have to put all your training and schooling together in an effective manner so that you can bring your horse to the fences in the balanced, rhythmical stride that you have created through your hard work on the flat. Keep in your mind's eye a picture of your horse, cantering in rhythm and balance, with you sitting in balance; your horse listening, waiting and responding to each aid; your horse jumping the first fence and landing without rushing off; your horse taking three or four strides to the next fence without increasing or decreasing his speed and jumping the next fence in exactly the same manner. This is the picture you are now going to create. This is how show jumps stay up and don't come tumbling down! Always picture yourself doing things well – never imagine doing things wrong – or you will end up doing them wrong. This is known as 'positive visualisation'.

A question of balance

How does riding a horse who is out of balance feel? Terrible! He will generally pull down on to his forehand, falling in on his shoulder or drifting out towards the outside shoulder. There is nothing quite so uncomfortable as trying to ride a horse to a fence when he is pulling down and dragging you out of the saddle and out of balance. A situation develops where there is no balance at all between you and your horse, leading to a lack of co-ordination and complete non-co-operation. Your horse will run to his fences with his weight on the forehand and then has to try to lift his shoulders up to jump the fence while the rest of his weight is trying to push his shoulders down.

Each time a horse jumps a fence he expends a great deal of power. He travels through the air at a considerable velocity and, if you have no control over that power, any problem you have will magnify quickly. Riding around a set of show jumps in a state of imbalance is accumulative. Each time your horse travels *into* a fence out of balance he will land out of it even more out of balance. There is a fine line between being in and out of balance, between having rhythm and lacking rhythm and being in or out of control. Repetition is the key to achieving many of the qualities required to keep it all together but unfortunately there is a tendency to replicate bad habits more easily than good ones.

How does riding a horse who is in balance feel? Wonderful! He comes to the fence with his weight in the hind legs, carrying himself forward with impulsion and at the correct speed. He jumps and lands in balance, not running away from you but just continuing at a correct and even pace. This is the situation you are striving to create.

The approach

The first point to make about the approach to the fence is that, in the show jumping arena, your approach to any fence is likely to come off a corner or immediately after another fence. You can teach your horse to jump in a straight line until you are blue in the face but he will not be any better equipped to compete. So when schooling at home, you should approach fences off circles, corners and from related distances (for more on related distances see Chapter 11), in both straight and curved lines.

The penultimate corner before a fence is the last moment in which you can make major adjustments. If they are not made then, then you have left it rather too late. The adjustments you should think about making include putting your horse in balance and making sure that, as he turns the corner, he is full square over his inside hind leg, pushing himself around the corner and not leaning heavily into your hand. You can make a half-halt before the corner, slow down before the corner, or encourage more forward movement in the corner. Whatever adjustment you make it must be made to ensure that your horse comes out of the corner with the right amount of activity, balance, rhythm and tempo. It is always your job to ensure that your horse is in balance. This requires speed, skill and a forward-thinking rider who has a good instinct for balance, a good firm position and a sound use of leg and hand.

The final approach to the fence begins at the last corner before it and it is from here that you have to develop the appropriate speed and impulsion for the fence or fences. Your horse's balance depends largely on what speed you are travelling at and, as it is the height and width of the fence you are jumping that should govern that speed, it stands to reason that you need to adapt the canter to suit the fence you are approaching. If you are jumping a vertical fence, you may need to approach it a little more slowly but if you are jumping a great big wide triple bar, you are not going to want to walk into it!

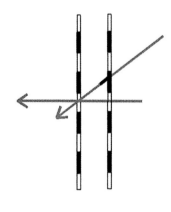

Jumping straight and at an angle. At the beginning of your horse's training he should be encouraged to jump straight across his fences. If he jumps crookedly he has further to travel across the fence, because it effectively becomes wider. Later on in his career, when he needs to win in jump-off situations, he will have to learn to jump across fences at an angle.

You must ride according to what you think the horse's reaction to the fence is going to be when you get to it. A big, wide fence is likely to make your horse back off, whereas a straight vertical will not, so you have to do a certain amount of the backing-off. You will need to contain your horse in the hand more, coming to the vertical, than you will coming to the oxer, where you are travelling in a more forward manner so that your horse meets it with a forward-thinking stride, making the ground up to clear all the parts of the fence.

Once you have put your horse in balance through the corners and have straightened him up from the final corner to the fence you are approaching, there should be no more corrections to make. However, the problem with riding a bad corner is that it will lead to a bad approach. If your horse comes to a fence off a corner, out of balance and too much on his forehand, his weight will be thrown on to the outside shoulder; he will jump the fence at too sharp an angle and will drift outwards across the fence. If you make a bad approach to a fence, all you can do is hold your horse together between hand and leg and rely on his goodwill and natural ability to get you over it. If your horse is drifting badly across the fence he will need to have even more natural ability, as the obstacle he is jumping will be a wider one than the course builder intended it to be.

If your approach hasn't worked out as you had planned, you need to have contingency plans. A rider who is *habitually* turning corners badly should not be in the competition arena but should go back to square one, sorting out the horse's balance on the flat, before entering the arena again. However, things can go wrong *on occasion* on the approach to a fence and, if this happens, you may need to adapt a 'seat of the pants' style of riding – that is to say, if things start to go drastically wrong then your 'instinctive' skill needs to kick in.

Two contrasting jumps at the start of a related distance. The photo (below left) shows the horse jumping forward and strong. The rider is sitting slightly behind him and using his weight to help the horse's balance. The photo (below right) shows a very calm, well balanced take-off so the rider can give his full attention to the next fence.

As explained further below, 'instinctive skill' is just that – it is not a panic reaction! In such circumstances, it is no good just kicking and hoping, or just pulling on the reins, because the latter will just make your horse hollow. You must use your reins *and* your legs to initiate a bigger, rounder canter stride – and you must practise this at home. Try to practise coming into a fence a little too fast, thus creating a situation in which the horse is going to land flat, so that you can learn to round him up on the landing stride and produce the powerful, balanced canter you need to jump the next fence in good style.

Psychologically, the approach to the next fence begins when you are actually in the air over the fence you are jumping. Physically, the approach starts as the horse puts his first foot on the ground during landing. You should be thinking in the air about the type of approach and jump you have just achieved. If your approach was a good, balanced one and the jump you are doing feels right and your horse is in a good, round bascule then your landing is likely to be balanced, as is your movement away from the fence and the approach to the next. If your horse has powered into the fence, has made a flat trajectory over it and lands running on his forehand, then you will need to bring him back into balance before the next fence.

The ideal situation is that your horse lands over every fence in a steady rhythm, carrying himself without effort; that he does not slow down or speed up without being asked to do so – in short, he allows you to ride him. Corrections and improvements are progressive – you will not make everything happen all at the same time. You will have setbacks, so it is important not to get too hung up about it. Horses have to learn gradually.

Planning and instinct

Try to operate on two levels – within your *plan* and *instinctively*. When you set up an exercise or walk a show jumping course you should have a plan of how you are going to approach each fence. The first time your horse will have ever seen these fences is when you are asking him to jump them, so make sure that you have planned 'how' you are going to ask him to jump them. You must make a clear, determined effort to walk the course properly so that you can plan precisely what you are going to do. Once you have made your plan, you must stick to it as far as is possible. As American World War II commander General Patten one said: 'A good plan, executed half well, is better than no plan at all.' My version of this is: If you make a plan things *may* go wrong; if you do not have a plan things *will* go wrong!

The *planning* aspect requires that you study the course, walk it, then think about it and ride it in your mind before you ride it on your horse. Think about all the things that 'might' go wrong. Ask yourself how you will prevent things from going wrong and how you are going to react if they 'do' go wrong. This may sound like an awful lot of rigmarole to go through to jump a few poles, but it is important to remember that if you have a plan you will feel more in control of the situation and this feeling of control and confidence will be transmitted to your horse.

Thinking *instinctively* still requires that you know what is happening, *when* it is happening, so that you are able to react quickly and efficiently to circumstances. If your horse lands short over a fence and is not appearing to make any ground then you might try to kick and gallop forward to the next fence – *instinctive* but not *effective*! Your horse will flatten and become unbalanced for the approach to the next fence. To be both *instinctive* and *effective* you need to think 'balance, rhythm and tempo' all the time. So, when your horse lands flat you have to 'instinctively' drive him forward with your legs, into strong, restraining hands. This will collect his hind legs underneath you so you are putting all his power and weight back into his quarters – where it needs to be – to return to a well-balanced, round canter. You need to keep your hand off the panic button, which takes confidence and self-discipline. Confidence and discipline come with practice, repetition, training and planning.

If an instinctive rider is also planning correctly, things will work out. Instinct will tell this rider quickly when things are going wrong. An instinctive rider with quick reactions will have even more time in which to plan the next move. The more quickly a rider thinks, the more time there will be to react and adjust.

POINTS TO PONDER... Absolutely refuse to carry the horse.

Improving balance on landing

An exercise to improve your horse's balance on the landing stride is to use four fences in a long line with three- to five-stride distances between them. The fences need not be very large, in fact if they are quite small your horse may land flat and running to begin with and that is exactly the problem this exercise is designed to solve. Start with the fences at 0.90m (3ft) and raise them, as your horse progresses, up to 1.15m (3ft 9in).

Your aim is to approach all the fences in exactly the same rhythm and tempo each time and to monitor the quality of each jump. If your horse jumps the first in a flat manner and lands heavily on his forehand, the chances are that he will run in an unbalanced manner to the second. To avoid this you must be ready to bring him to a halt as soon as he has landed over the first fence. The reason for bringing the horse to a halt is to gain his full attention and to start making him think about what he is doing. The next time you jump the line your horse will be a little more careful about how he jumps each fence, but the momentum of jumping three or

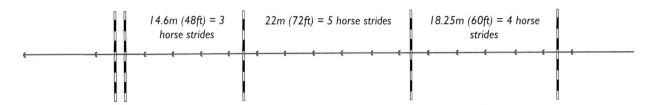

14.6m (48ft) = 3 horse strides   22m (72ft) = 5 horse strides   18.25m (60ft) = 4 horse strides

Exercise using a line of four fences (see text above). Approach all the fences in the same tempo and rhythm.

four fences may begin to make him flat again, so it is probable that you will have to stop him again after the third or fourth fence. You may have to repeat this exercise several times to focus your horse's mind on what you are doing.

Sometimes this 'pulling up' exercise is not all that pretty – that doesn't matter – what does is that it is functional. It has absolutely no function if you allow your horse to run on past fences rather than halt in a straight line or jump the fence in control. It is important that when you ask for the halt your horse halts, but this does not mean that you try to pull his back teeth out! The benefits of the exercise are that your horse should become attentive and should be listening to every single aid that you give him. The aim of the exercise is that your horse should be able to return to a state of balance each time he lands over a fence and so arrive at the next fence in balance as well.

Balancing act

Another good 'balancing act' is to practise initiating turns in the air. This helps your horse to land on the correct lead and also helps him establish his balance after the jump. It also gives your horse something to think about and lessens the chances of him rushing off on the landing stride. If you repeat an exercise a few times your horse will start to anticipate the next move. In this exercise we use the horse's anticipation to benefit his training.

If you initiate a turn to the right whilst in the air, three or four times, your horse will begin to anticipate that bend to the right and will start shifting his weight to the right in mid-air, landing with his right leg leading. If, however, during your next jump you initiate a turn to the left, your horse, with his weight already loaded to the right, will land lightly on his left leg and shoulder, putting him in better balance. The anticipation has helped you because your horse has put his weight on to the right shoulder and you have immediately taken it off the right shoulder, putting him on to a left lead, so he will be light in the left shoulder.

As with every jumping exercise you undertake, as you make the approach, monitor your canter and consider the condition of your horse's stride. He should be going forward with impulsion, be 'in front of the leg' and feel comfortable in the rein contact. On the last stride you must think about the moves you need to make. As your horse starts to take off you must look into the turn with your head up. Your eyes are important – make sure that they are looking in the direction that you intend to travel. Start the bend with an open, turning rein and increase the weight in your inside stirrup. However, don't exaggerate leaning into the turn or your weight on the inside will push your horse in the opposite direction. Moving your hand to an open rein position and turning your head are likely to create sufficient weight adjustment, into the inside stirrup, for your horse to follow. Your rein is leading your horse into the bend, not pulling him into it. If you try to pull your horse into the bend he is likely to set his jaw against you and run straight ahead, away from the blocking hand.

In both this and the previous exercise you should ride in the forward, balanced seat with your weight just off the saddle. This is important because you don't want your weight to influence the forward movement of your horse. What your weight 'must' influence is balance. If your weight is continually rocking backwards and forwards, your horse's balance and attention will be disturbed by these shifts and he won't be able to discern your aids.

Practise every skill you think you will need at home. Practise turning into corners and halting; riding through corners; turning out of corners; swinging corners; riding through corners without changing the rhythm or tempo; short turns that you are going to need in a jump-off; half-halts; halting from canter and cantering from halt – practise everything. Without this work at home you will not be able to perform in the arena.

Related Distances

WE SAY THAT FENCES are connected by a related distance when two or more are close enough together that the way you jump the first is going to directly affect the way you are able to jump the following fence(s). A related distance can be as short as one stride from the previous fence, or as far away as six or seven – or even ten strides. However, most people consider any fences placed between one and five strides apart to be related. They can be placed in a straight line or on a curved line (commonly called a 'dogleg'): I prefer to use the term 'curved line', as the curve may be shallow or sharp and can be described as necessary.

There are several things that may influence how a related distance is tackled. The two most important words to remember are 'balance' and 'tempo'. If you are out of balance and riding too fast as you approach and jump the first part of a related distance, you will land running on the forehand and be further out of balance as you approach and jump the second part. If you approach the fences too slowly and your horse makes too steep an arc over the first part, he will land too short for the second part, so you will have to start kicking like mad and then you are back in the first scenario, approaching the second part too fast and out of balance.

The factor that decides the speed at which you are going to approach the first part of a related distance is its format. Is it a vertical to an oxer? An oxer to a vertical? A vertical to a double, or an oxer to a double? Perhaps it is a treble combination? All of these things must be thought out when you walk the course and pace the distances between fences. You study and make a plan. The correct tempo depends entirely on the fences and the distances between them. If the distance is rather long, then you will have to approach the first part a little bit more quickly than if the distance seemed spot on or too short. That way you will land moving forward just a fraction, making the distance suitable for your horse to take off for the second part in balance. If the distance seems far too long then it will be necessary for you to make the horse put in an extra stride to get to the second part in balance.

When the horse takes off in balance he will land in balance and continue through the related distance in equally good balance to jump the next fence.

TIM STOCKDALE

Riders should try to produce as much rhythm in their work as possible. If you can maintain a good rhythm when you are cantering and jumping a course then everything will seem a lot sweeter. If you are continually increasing and decreasing your tempo, and if your transitions are jerky and harsh, then ultimately your job will be a lot harder.

Be aware of what your horse is doing underneath you. Once you begin to concentrate on your rhythm you will become aware of his stride pattern and what his legs are doing. As a result of this you will begin to feel that your horse's legs are an extension of you and that is the whole purpose of riding – that the horse and rider are one.

Olympic and European team member, winner of the King George V Gold Cup and one of the UK's top riders and coaches.

The problem for riders

Many riders will have a problem with adjusting their horse's stride because horses learn to run forward, especially if they have been kicked forward initially. The show jumping rider has to be able to lengthen and shorten the stride almost instantaneously because, as you have already learned, the show jumper must have an 'infinitely adjustable' stride. Often, during the cross-country phase of eventing, the most important thing the horse has to be able to do is to lengthen his stride, not shorten it. Traditionally, event riders tended to put all their eggs in one basket and ride forward to every fence in the hope that a horse, taught in this fashion, would be able to deal with fences by standing off them. However, this has changed dramatically over the last few years; cross-country riding is now far more technical and the riders need a greater degree of adjustability owing to the larger number of 'skinnies' and multiple combinations of jumps.

Adding a stride between two fences is a very skilful thing to do because it requires using your hands, legs and bodyweight to influence the length of the horse's stride, the take-off stride and the way the horse jumps. When you use your hands, legs and bodyweight to make the stride shorter you are effecting a very subtle half-halt. However the difference between the half-halt that we talked about when working the horse on the flat and this half-halt is that now, once you have achieved the shortened stride asked for by the half-halt, you are going to maintain it all the way to the next fence, so that each stride will be in balance and more active.

What you don't want to do is allow your horse to run more quickly to the fence and then suddenly panic and make the adjustment on the last stride, as that last stride will be weak and hesitant instead of being a perfect one. If you allow your horse to run to the fence, making an adjustment in the last stride, one of many things will happen. He could crash straight through the fence, or stop, or he may jump in an inverted style, taking poles with him, or he may duck out at the last moment. Always in show jumping you are striving to make the take-off stride

The mathematics of related distances.

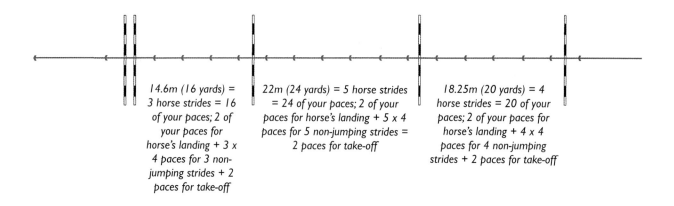

14.6m (16 yards) = 3 horse strides = 16 of your paces; 2 of your paces for horse's landing + 3 x 4 paces for 3 non-jumping strides + 2 paces for take-off

22m (24 yards) = 5 horse strides = 24 of your paces; 2 of your paces for horse's landing + 5 x 4 paces for 5 non-jumping strides = 2 paces for take-off

18.25m (20 yards) = 4 horse strides = 20 of your paces; 2 of your paces for horse's landing + 4 x 4 paces for 4 non-jumping strides + 2 paces for take-off

perfect, so the ingredients for that stride – the balance, impulsion, speed and rhythm – all have to be blended precisely. If all the strides are exactly the same length approaching the fence, then the horse will be able to take off in balance.

This issue of adjusting stride can be a very tough problem to solve and the solutions may seem, at first, to need rather a tough attitude. If, when practising at home, your horse jumps the first fence in a related distance and then runs blindly forward you must pull up to a halt, as described in the previous chapter. He must be taught that he is not allowed to run on unthinkingly and that he must listen and pay attention to you at all times. You may have to do this two or three times before your horse gets the message. The first couple of times may not be a very pretty sight; your horse may throw his head up or down, cross his jaw or swing his quarters but he must pay attention when he lands over that first part of the related distance. Remember that horses react more quickly than we do, so in order to facilitate any change in the horse's stride pattern, we have to really speed up our own reaction time. There is no particular exercise to help with this except to practise and learn to concentrate on and develop intuition and feel.

Making a plan

Planning for the arena

With a young horse it is desirable to teach him all the attributes mentioned previously; namely to shorten or lengthen his stride between two fences whilst always remaining in balance. If you and your horse are in harmony and balance when you land over the first part of a related distance then 99 per cent of the time you will clear the second part, so try to keep two things in mind when training. First, plan and have a clear idea in your own mind what you intend to do. In 'planning mode' everything is orderly and organised in your head. You know what you're going to do and how you're going to react to everything, according to your plan. If circumstances change, resulting in your plan not coming to fruition, you must react instinctively as you land over the fence, to ensure that you are back on track as soon as possible.

So, if your plans do go awry, a quick, instinctive reaction is desirable. You must learn to act on instinct and make that instinct *work* for you. So if you have planned to take five strides to the next fence but your horse has landed a little steep and is running, you must react instinctively. This means you must learn to feel what's happening automatically, to know when things are wrong and to know, without thinking, precisely what you need to do to put things right again. Your instinct should have started to kick in almost before your horse took off because you will have felt him lose control on that important last stride and you will have therefore realised that he is going to land out of balance. You need to be thinking and reacting instinctively while your horse is still in the air, so that you are mentally and physically ready to act as soon as he lands. That's a lot of instinct, isn't it, but that's what good riding is all about, so stay sharp.

Practise at home

To be able to plan and to think instinctively takes time and practice and you must learn to speed your brain up. How do you do it? Well, you can't enter a competition and say to yourself: 'Today, I am going to think really quickly.' You must try at home to consider as many scenarios as possible and then try to think of ways in which you will cope with each one. Practise approaching the first part of a related distance at different speeds and different lengths of stride, to make the distance vary. Then adjust the stride pattern in the distance accordingly.

You can assume that any course in a competition arena is made up of several different exercises linked together to make a complete challenge for both horse and rider. So if you practise as many of those exercises as you can at home then you aren't going to be taken by surprise when you do get into the arena.

In the beginning, the way to practise related distances is not to set up huge oxers at difficult distances but to put up very small fences and vary the distances between them. You can start off with as many strides as you wish, but I suggest four non-jumping strides to begin with. Start off by putting a pole on the ground and measuring the distance between it and another pole placed either on a straight or curved line. Measure the distance in multiples of four of your normal strides, which should be approximately 0.9m (3ft) long – each of your four strides equating to one horse stride. As you will rarely have a tape measure with you, try to learn how to pace out distances evenly; this, of course, requires you to know, to a fair degree of accuracy, the actual length of your strides. It is no good striding out in multiples of four of your normal steps if your normal paces are only 0.6m (2ft), or if they are 1.05m (3ft 5in) long, as the whole project will be thrown into disarray and your horse will become very confused! Educate yourself in any way you see fit. You can cut a length of wood to 0.9m (3ft) long and teach yourself that from the back of one heel to the front of your other toe, as you take a stride, is exactly that length, or you can mark a path at 0.9m (3ft) intervals so that you can get into rhythm. Whichever way you choose, the end result will be that you can walk every distance on every course in exactly the same way.

Now, back to our poles. This exercise is similar to those suggested in Chapter 9 but it does have some subtle differences. Ensure that the poles are easily approachable and that the going underfoot is good. We have two poles on the ground with four (as a suggested starting point), five or six strides in between them. As you canter your horse over the two poles, see how many strides he takes to cover the ground between them in his normal stride pattern. (When cantering through a curved line it is important that you canter straight through the middle of the curve, aiming for the centre of the poles and riding the curve as you have planned to.) Later on you can practise taking the short or long line to alter the distance between the poles, but not yet.

When jumping related distances on a curve it is essential that you have walked the distance and assessed how you are going to ride the curve; you can't leave it to luck. Walk the distance, look back and see where you have come from and look forward and see where you are going, so you can decide where the curve is going to start and finish. The most important thing to remember, when riding a curved line, is that as soon as you are in the air over the first fence, your eye should be locked on to the second. Another way that you can teach yourself to ride correctly through a related distance is to make a passage through the curve using poles and a cone as shown in the diagram on pages 141 and 142. This gives you an opportunity to find a true line.

Planning your route. There is more than one route through a curved line, but fences in a straight line do not give you 'options'.

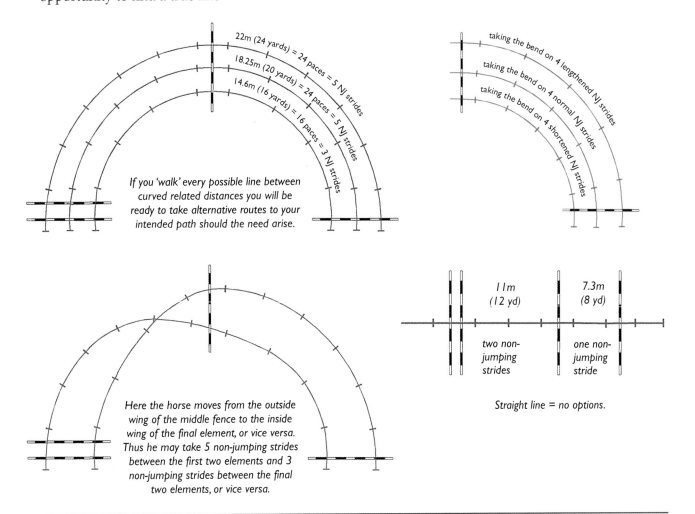

22m (24 yards) = 24 paces = 5 NJ strides
18.25m (20 yards) = 24 paces = 5 NJ strides
14.6m (16 yards) = 16 paces = 3 NJ strides

If you 'walk' every possible line between curved related distances you will be ready to take alternative routes to your intended path should the need arise.

taking the bend on 4 lengthened NJ strides
taking the bend on 4 normal NJ strides
taking the bend on 4 shortened NJ strides

Here the horse moves from the outside wing of the middle fence to the inside wing of the final element, or vice versa. Thus he may take 5 non-jumping strides between the first two elements and 3 non-jumping strides between the final two elements, or vice versa.

11m (12 yd) — two non-jumping strides

7.3m (8 yd) — one non-jumping stride

Straight line = no options.

Long-striding horses

If you have set up a distance of five strides and your horse covers this in four massive, uncontrolled strides then you know you are going to be in deep trouble when you start to jump fences on a related distance. If your horse comes into this category – in other words he has long, raking strides – you will have to put together an exercise to shorten his stride. You need to gain his attention after the first pole. To do this, canter over the first pole and bring him to a halt about three or four strides later. Bring him around again and this time, ask him to halt within two or three strides of the first pole. Your aim through this exercise is to make your horse pay attention to the aids, so that he does not go blindly on whether the poles are there or not. Once you have his attention you can almost disregard the poles and concentrate on shortening his stride. Get as many strides in between the two poles as you can. As his canter becomes rounder, shorter and more engaged then the adjustment between the two poles is going to become easier.

Even then your long-striding horse may still have a basic preference to stand off his fences and to jump them with a big, bold jump, rather than getting in close and making an athletic jump – but he has to learn to get in deep to fences otherwise he will be in trouble as they increase in size. What you do now with poles on the ground at home will be very influential as the fences get bigger and wider. These simple exercises help to build the confidence and knowledge base of both you and your horse. If you know that you can shorten your horse's stride at home you will have the confidence to do so in the arena and, as your horse becomes accustomed to you asking him to do different things with his stride, he won't panic when you ask for a quick shortening of his stride during a competition.

Short-striding horses

The alternative reaction to the horse who takes long strides through the initial poles exercise is the horse who puts in six or seven very short strides: with him, you know that you're going to have to make some adjustments as the obstacles become bigger and wider. However, it must be stressed that a shorter stride is infinitely more desirable than a long, flat stride. Therefore, if your horse fits into this category you don't want to alter him a *great deal*. He probably has a naturally springy stride which is desirable for show jumping but, if we assume that your horse has sufficient talent and you have sufficient talent, enthusiasm and ambition to progress in show jumping, then you need to be sure that he is 'infinitely adjustable'.

Although they can be used with good effect with any horse, canter poles are of particular benefit to the horse with a short stride. This time we try to take a stride *out* when cantering between poles. Once you have landed over the first you could flap the reins and kick to lengthen your horse's stride, but although you may achieve this you are more likely to turn him into a nervous wreck or, at the least, turn his nice, bouncy stride into a flat, hurried one. What you really need to do, to lengthen his stride, is to use lots of canter poles. Most riders don't like riding over canter poles as it makes their stride absolutely committed, leaving them no chance to adjust it, so we use the canter poles for that precise reason. It is very easy to allow the short-striding horse to shorten his stride still further because that is comfortable, but when you ask him to lengthen his stride, it can be uncomfortable.

Place the canter poles 3m (9ft 9in) apart. This encourages the horse to make a slightly lengthened stride between each pole. As time goes on you can widen the distance between the poles slightly, up to a distance of 3.2m (10ft 6in), to produce a fairly ideal, bold stride that is ready to take on bigger fences. You may scratch your head and say: 'Well, he said that an ideal stride is 3.65m (12ft) long and here he is saying that a 3.2m (10ft 6in) stride is ideal; something doesn't add up somewhere!'

Remember that you are trying to adjust your horse 'by degrees', so it would be very foolish of you to place the poles 3.65m (12ft) apart when your horse has a 2.75m (9ft) stride. Be content to see your horse lengthen from the short stride up to a 3.35m (11ft) stride, which is sufficiently long to get you through most combinations. Once your horse has accepted that he is able to lengthen his stride when required and you are comfortable riding him through those lengthened strides, the rest of the adjustment needed to make 3.65m (12ft) strides will be created by the horse's natural enthusiasm and by the adrenalin on tap once in the ring. You are not making it normal for your short-striding horse to go through every distance on a long stride; you are simply creating an element of adjustment that may be necessary occasionally during the horse's jumping career. You are trying to make the horse's habit of going short into a more flexible one of being adjustable.

Progressing

Once you are cantering between the two poles and are easily able to shorten or lengthen your horse's stride as much as is practical, it is time to raise the poles to create two small fences of approximately 0.45m (1ft 6in), to make this into a jumping exercise. The important thing to remember now is 'do not change anything' and then 'nothing will change'. If you approach the poles in exactly the same way then you can do exactly the same exercise. As you become confident with the poles at this height, you can begin to increase the complexity of the exercise by gradually increasing the height further; by changing the related distance; by introducing oxers and spreads; and by adding a double combination at the end of the related distance.

Then it is time to put your homework to the test by stringing several of your different exercises together. You can do this in a field when the going underfoot is good or in a 20 x 40m arena. You should construct a three-stride distance to a four-stride distance then have a curved line to a five-stride distance with, perhaps, a double at the end. Then you can come back over the same course, having your double combination as your first fence. All the time you are educating yourself to ride as clearly and as positively as you can to the level, measured distance, but you should always be acutely aware that if your horse falters or makes a mistake, you must be ready to adjust his stride so that he arrives at the next fence in balance.

If you are riding from an oxer to a vertical you will have to approach the oxer with a little more power and you are going to have to be ready to make a quick adjustment to your horse's stride as soon as he has landed. Because the vertical is less imposing your horse will be less likely to respect it and more likely to take off too close to it, taking out the top rail with his forelegs. To make him respect the vertical you have to make a shortening adjustment to his stride and you will have to mentally prepare for that adjustment while you are in the air.

In the reverse situation, if you are riding from a vertical to an oxer, most of the time you will approach the vertical with caution and a slightly slower stride. Then you will need to put an enormous amount of power into the first stride after landing, so that the horse is moving forward with sufficient activity in his stride and sufficient enthusiasm in his mind to jump the oxer.

All of these exercises need to be practised time and time again before you go to your first show – not after you have made your first big mistakes in public. Then related distance riding will not become that awful thing that you see where the rider attacks the fences blindly and storms through the distance, regardless of what it is. If you can make your horse confident with related distances, he will eventually teach himself that they are easy to go to and jump.

To gain your horse's confidence can take many months but to lose it can take seconds!

Jumping Combinations

MANY YEARS AGO in Novice competitions the only double combination you would come across would be one double of uprights. They were only there to introduce the horse to the idea of jumping two fences together. But time marches on and as riders, horses, technique and training improve, so that even at a Novice level people are more capable, you are usually expected to jump two double combinations consisting of oxers, triple bars or uprights.

The combinations that you will come across most frequently are either doubles or trebles, each with a distance of no more than 11m (36ft) between them. In some exceptional circumstances, competitions contain quadruple combinations made up of four obstacles with a distance of no more than 11m (36ft) between them. The approach to any combination requires all the ingredients that we have already talked about in our work on the flat, namely rhythm, impulsion, balance and an approach to the fence at the correct speed – and it also requires calmness.

The distances between elements in a combination are formulaic: maximum and minimum distances for any given combination at any height are set down in the *B.S. Course Builder's Manual*. Nearly every course builder sets out to build a good combination, as to build a trick combination would be to lay themselves wide open to accusations of setting out to maim and destroy the confidence of the horses. How each horse covers each distance will vary greatly, depending on several factors. Muddy conditions, an uphill slope, a cramped arena and jumping away from home can shorten a horse's stride by up to 0.3m (1ft). Springy turf, jumping towards home, a gentle downhill slope and a spacious arena can lengthen the stride by the same distance. Even the colour of the combination may have an effect on how it is jumped, so it is essential to watch other riders and see how their horses cope with the distances.

One of the greatest mistakes made by riders jumping combinations is to believe that the faster they go in, the more likely they are to come out the other side. Unfortunately all that really happens is that the horse becomes more and more unbalanced, resulting in a heavy shower of dislodged poles! If, because of your anxiety, your horse comes to the first fence in a long, flat, hurried stride then he will take off in a low, long trajectory and, whether or not he lowers a pole, he will land on his forehand. He then has only one or two strides in which to pick himself up, ready to jump the next fence. If he is already travelling too fast and heavily on his forehand then he is going to have a massive problem getting himself organised and back on to his hocks to jump the second fence, and the problems are going to be greatly multiplied if there is a third element.

An important point to remember is that you cannot jump out until you have jumped in. 'Of course you can't jump out until you jump in!' comes a universal cry but my point is that you cannot jump out, *in balance*, unless you have jumped in *in balance*. So you must first address getting into the combination. Presumably you will have walked the course before you attempt to jump it so you know the distance between the fences (if you don't, then you are leaving yourself open to problems that should have been avoided). As you pace out the distance between the fences you should also assess the type of combination you will be jumping: for example, is it a vertical to an oxer, an oxer to a vertical, or a triple bar to an oxer to a vertical? Your approach to the combination should correspond with whatever the 'going in' part is, be it a vertical or an oxer. What happens after that, you have to deal with as it occurs. A double or treble combination is just a very short related distance, so how you jump the 'in' part will directly affect how you jump the next one or two parts.

A big oxer will ride even bigger as part of a combination because the horse will see the fence behind it and will be backing off the first fence, so you will have to approach the first fence with a small increase of speed and a large increase in activity. Knowing that the fence is coming, you need to build the canter and stride to suit the particular fence you are approaching. Hopefully the course builder will have taken this into account and made the distance between the two fences short enough to allow the horse to back off, land a little short and steep and still make the distance to the second fence.

The real secret to jumping a combination well is to jump in correctly and you will then jump through the combination correctly.

Know the way to the fence

I try to stress to my riders that they should know, on the way to the fence, how their horse is feeling so that, one or two strides away, they will know whether he is going forward and is taking the fence on, or is backing off and withdrawing his labour. Whatever feel you get from your horse on the way to the fence, you must do something about it as quickly as possible, so if you feel the horse backing off the combination you must try to put a little more enthusiasm into his stride so that you know he is moving into your hand. It is always better to have your horse taking you to the fence than having to kick. He should not be pulling your arms out but he should, at least, be as enthusiastic about getting to the fence as you are and, hopefully, be twice as enthusiastic as you are! There is nothing worse than coming to a fence when you are full of enthusiasm but your horse has no enthusiasm for the job at all. You will end up approaching the fence kicking hard and thinking: 'Oh my God, this is going to be a complete disaster!' On the other hand, if your horse is moving forward in an enthusiastic manner and you are coming to the fence thinking: 'This feels good', then you know that you are going to be able to deal with almost anything.

Once you are in a combination you will know what you have to do to get out, but before you get in, you spend a few milliseconds in the air. As the horse takes off, assess that take-off as he clears the fence; assess the shape of jump the horse has produced and where you are going to land. If you think: 'Yes that was a good take-off, this is a good jump and we are going to land in the right spot', then there is little else to do to prepare for the next fence, but if you think: 'Help, we are going to land short', then you know that you are going to have to kick. If you think: 'We are going to land too near to the next fence', then you know that you are going to have to take a pull. You have to react when you have jumped the fence, before you land – your brain has got to be working in advance of everything. The more quickly you think, the more time you have in which to react. I liken it to skidding on ice, whether in a car or on a bicycle. Everything seems to go into slow motion – but it doesn't, the world isn't slowing down but your brain is speeding up; it overtakes the situation and plans your reactions

Technically, treble combinations don't take any more jumping than double combinations but your horse may back off more, daunted by seeing so many poles and colour in front of him. In Novice competitions the combination should always be built to encourage the horse to jump. An ascending oxer to a vertical is the most inviting combination, as opposed to a square oxer to a vertical, or a vertical to an oxer. A sensible course builder will put the filler in the first element of a combination but you do get bad course designers who will put the filler under the second or third elements and use poles on the first fence. This will direct the horse's eye straight through the poles to the filler, encouraging him to ignore the first element – not good, especially for a novice horse.

Combination training

When it comes to training your horse to jump combinations, like everything else related to training him, keep it simple. Make everything very straightforward at home so that at no time does the horse suffer knock-backs. It is important to give your horse tasks that he can do easily, so that he will come back for more; if you keep asking him to do the impossible he is very likely to throw down his tools. However, you must be progressive.

All young horses jump differently. Some will be very cautious and green and will jump very high with gangly, dangling legs; others will be a lot braver and will carry on regardless so that by the time you reach the fourth fence you are flying. The brave horse may be easier to train through combinations but he may not always leave every fence standing. The cautious, careful horse who is loath to touch a fence may take more time and may be more difficult to train through combinations, but he is going to clear them.

I start by building a small line of three or four fences of approximately 0.45m (1ft 6in), so that the horse gets used to seeing a line of jumps. Once he is used to seeing a line of fences you can start to build wider and higher. It is important to be careful with the distances because you must not make them so long that the horse begins to flatten, nor so short that he is tempted to try to bounce the distance in between each fence. When you are building small combinations, you should ensure that the distance between each fence will encourage your horse to make a nice, rounded jump over each. Vary the poles between one-stride (7m/23ft) and two-stride (10.2m/33ft 6in) distances.

Although modern-day show jumping is conducted primarily on prepared artificial surfaces, when we are jumping on grass, which most event riders have to do, then as the height of the fences increases, so should the distance between them. A rule of thumb is to increase the distance by 15cm (6in) for every 15cm (6in) of height, but always take your conditions into account. As mentioned earlier, mud and jumping uphill can shorten your horse's stride by up to 30cm (1ft) whereas good turf and gentle downhill slopes can increase it by the same amount. A combination of particular conditions – for example, jumping uphill in heavy going – may influence stride length even more than this. Jumping towards or away from home and the amount of space you are jumping in can also affect length of stride.

Start by building your line of fences purely with poles. I like to introduce fillers at the sides of the jump, acting much like wings, so that the horse gets used to

Safe distances for canter poles. Always measure canter poles backwards from the first rail of the fence you are jumping, never forwards from the fence you have jumped.

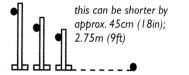

this can be shorter by approx. 45cm (18in); 2.75m (9ft)

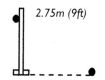

2.75m (9ft)

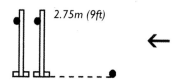

2.75m (9ft)

seeing them without actually having to jump them. As he becomes used to them you can gradually move them in towards the centre of the fence.

If your horse is very bold and is running through the line of fences, getting closer and closer to each one, then put a pole in between each fence to draw his eye down to the ground so that he makes a deliberate stride and is in a better position to jump the fence. Conversely, you don't want masses of poles on the ground for your timid horse, as it is likely to make him more anxious. However, as the timid horse becomes more forward-going then I would put the poles on the ground and lengthen the distances between each fence to encourage him to move forward through the distance. The pole should be measured from the *next fence* you are going to jump, not the one you are jumping.

Don't be tempted to skip the basics with your tremendously talented, scopey horse just because he 'is' tremendously talented and has amazing scope to his jump. All horses will eventually 'hit a wall' and once that happens it is tremendously difficult to get over unless you have done the groundwork. If the horse is not completely happy jumping three or four fences in a row and taking them well within his stride then, when you do hit a problem, such as a difficult combination, your horse is going to be frightened and will be backing off before you jump the first fence. But if you've done all your homework he may hesitate and take a look but the basic idea in his head will be that he goes forward and takes on the fence.

Speed is not the answer

Always remember that speed is not the answer, although it is a trap that we all fall into at one time or another. I remember riding a young horse through a treble combination and as he approached the third element he ran out, in fact he had actually been backing off during the approach. I brought him towards the combination a second time with a lot more speed and he backed off more and still ran out. As time went on I learned through experience that the correct way to deal with this situation would have been to redress the balance and create more controlled energy and this would have given the horse more confidence in me and a more reliable canter to jump from. If this happens during a competition then the answer is to touch your hat, retire gracefully and go home and practise. In that instance the horse was not ready to jump that particular combination with that sort of canter.

Another mistake that a large number of riders make is to bully their horses through combinations when they just aren't ready to jump them. If your horse is making mistakes through combinations it doesn't necessarily mean that he needs to be punished. So often horses make mistakes in combinations because they are genuinely frightened and, if you hit a horse for being frightened, it will just increase the fear. Once a horse gets combination phobia he just has to turn a corner and see a combination to start back-pedalling.

Gymnastic Jumping

GYMNASTIC EXERCISES are very important and will teach you and your horse several things. Jumping a grid on a schoolmaster will help you, as a rider, with your confidence, balance and position. Their primary function for the horse is to improve his technique as well as developing his gymnastic ability and power. It is essential to aim the exercises at the level of skill that the horse has attained. However, grids can also be a trainer's cop-out. So often a show jumping lesson can just turn into a gridwork session and overdoing gridwork is just as retrograde a step as not doing any at all.

A simple grid

A very simple exercise for a horse at the beginning of his career, to teach him to go from one fence to another with enthusiasm and confidence, is to put a placing pole or three trotting poles in front of a small fence and then, a short distance away, (approximately 6.5m/21ft 4in) have another small fence. This exercise draws the horse's eye to the ground, makes him look where he is putting his feet and asks him to make two simple jumps. When the horse is comfortable jumping the two fences, you can put a back rail on the second part to make an oxer. This will get him in the air and soon he'll realise that he can actually jump a bigger fence.

This exercise can also be used to improve your horse's technique – especially his shoulder action – to increase his power and strength and to encourage him to bascule. As he becomes more confident, you can raise the second element and begin to draw the front rail gradually towards the first element, thus widening the oxer and shortening the distance between the two fences.

Taking this exercise to its ultimate conclusion, as it would be jumped by a very experienced horse, the highest I would make the fence would be approximately 1.10m (3ft 7in) and the distance between the two fences would shorten to 4.5m (14ft 9in), making the spread 1.83m (6ft) wide – quite a considerable fence. It is an exercise that should be undertaken with caution, but it has a two-fold effect:

1. It improves the bascule.
2. It encourages power jumping off the hind legs in a short distance. We are, in fact, 'condensing' the stride to jump the width, not increasing it.

The first step to successful gymnastic jumping is the raised trot pole. The horse is using himself with a powerful, elevated and athletic trot.

Grid to improve general technique. *Approach in trot.*

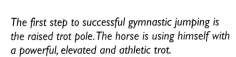

'Power Grid' *from trot, to generate more power.*

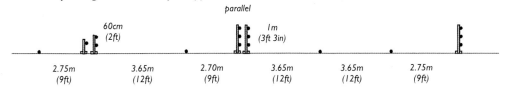

Bounce grid *from trot. Improves horse's balance, gives him confidence and sharpens his mind. Start with two fences (one bounce) and add one at a time.*

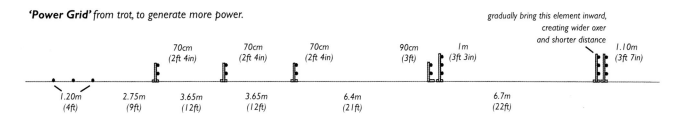

Canter grid *to improve your horse's foreleg action. Carefully move each side of the oxer outwards, widening the oxer and reducing the distance between each fence. Move each element of the oxer a maximum of 30cm (1ft).*

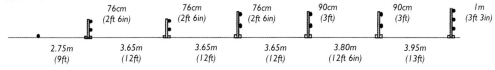

Trot grid *to improve hind leg action. Note that the back rail on the second ascending oxer is much higher than the front rail.*

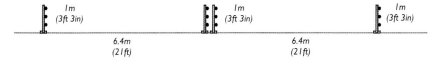

Bounce jumping

I also use bounce jumping quite frequently, either from trot or from canter. A bounce distance is one in which the horse has to take off for the second fence without taking a non-jumping stride after the first fence, which obviously entails an enormous amount of power, drive and athleticism. Bounce jumping exercises used to be looked down on by the show jumping fraternity but they are becoming more popular as their benefits are more widely understood. Because the horse has to *think* very quickly it is a good exercise for his mind and, because he has to *move* very quickly, it is a good exercise for his body. His shoulders have to come up very quickly and therefore his head goes down quickly. Because his shoulders go up and his neck goes down, his back comes up in the middle and this allows him to 'throw his hind legs away' from the fence in a correct manner. All in all, the bounce causes an awful lot of hinges, pulleys and levers to work very quickly in rapid succession.

Bounce fences can be very small, approximately 0.45–0.6m (1ft 6in–2ft) for the young horse or, for the more experienced horse, as high as 1m (3ft 3in). Try to imagine the strength and gymnastic ability required by a horse to bounce over a row of four or five fences at that height. Do not make the distance between each bounce any less than 2.65m (12ft); to make a bounce too short puts too much strain on the horse's joints, muscles and tendons.

Start off with two or three very small bounce fences in a row, but you must be careful with bounce fences because the horse can get confused and intimidated by a barrage of poles. A timid horse may jump two or three bounces yet, if confronted with two or three more, he may start panicking – touching a foot down in the wrong place or tripping over the fences. For such a horse you could make

Canter grid to improve the horse's scope. It is designed for an experienced horse. You can gradually widen the final oxer by moving both elements.

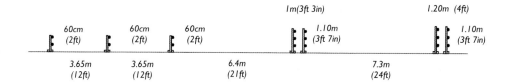

Canter grid using three raised poles. To improve the horse's 'vertical' jumping ability.

Canter grid to improve the horse's 'combination' jumping ability. Again, this grid is for the more experienced horse.

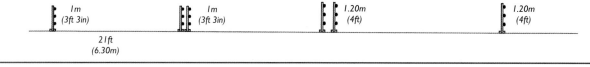

the fences even smaller, using poles raised 15cm (6in) off the ground – anything to make training simple, exciting and painless.

The power grid

One of my favourite exercises I call the 'power grid'. It simply consists of three bounce fences, one non-jumping stride to a fourth vertical and then a further non-jumping stride to either a square oxer or a descending oxer. (Although not used in competition the descending oxer is a useful and legitimate training aid that encourages the horse to be neater and sharper with his forelegs.)

Above top: The bounce grid will improve the horse's reaction and co-ordination.

Above: This is a useful grid used to develop power in the horse's jump by using a short distance between the elements.

General rules for creating a grid

These include:
- Do not put a bounce fence in the middle or at the end of a mixed grid.
- Build a grid that is within the capability of you and your horse.
- Distances that are made slightly short (30cm/1ft) encourage a horse to jump off his hocks, which is good.
- Distances that are too long (30cm/1ft) make a horse jump flat and on to his forehand, which is bad!
- If you want to make a bold horse more careful you can increase the number of obstacles in your grid.
- To provide a horse with one non-jumping stride the distance between fences should be between 7.15m and 7.9m (23ft 6in and 26ft).
- To provide a horse with two non-jumping strides the distance between fences should be between 10.45m and 10.8m (34ft 3in and 35ft 6in).
- The distance between two vertical fences can be shorter than the distance between a vertical and an oxer, or than between two oxers.
- Build your grid in a straight line.

- Always have an experienced person on the ground a) checking your distances and b) rebuilding knocked down fences.
- If you are using trotting poles make sure, if at all possible, they are stabilised in wooden blocks. If they are not, keep a sharp eye on them to make sure they are not moved.
- Trotting poles should be approximately 1.35m (4ft 6in) apart when used as an approach to a grid, but do need to be adjusted to suit the horse's gait.
- Trotting poles used on their own should be approximately 1.35m (4ft 6in) or 2.75m (9ft) apart.
- Canter poles on the approach to the grid should be 3m (9ft 9in) apart and should also, if possible, be stabilised in wooden blocks.

Finally, remember that any tool you can use to keep horse and rider safe is a good idea – the fewer mistakes you make the more quickly you will learn. Good practice develops confidence and making bad mistakes or letting people do unsafe or unwise things does not develop confidence. Good practice makes perfect.

A word on ground lines

Ground line poles should be used under every fence to encourage your horse to look down to the base of the jump and to discourage him from running in too close. It is a misconception to believe that a ground line frightens the horse off the pole or actively encourages him to stand off too much. When jumping verticals the ground line should always be at least 30cm (1ft) in front of the fence and, as the fence get higher, it can be pulled out further.

When jumping oxers the ground line pole need only be underneath the front rail and should only be pulled out occasionally if the horse needs to be encouraged to back off. Always place ground lines in front of, or under the fence, never behind it. A false ground line will trick your horse into thinking he must take off closer to the fence than he actually needs to, possibly leading to a nasty accident and almost certainly leading to a loss of confidence. Also remember that the more poles you use in a grid, the more daunting and difficult it may look to your horse. Confronted with such a maze of poles your horse may either misjudge where to put his feet or may just decide to go on strike.

Trying to teach your horse to show jump through trickery will not work, but providing him with a large knowledge base gives him plenty to fall back on. Familiarity breeds confidence. If you are training the horse with good gymnastic exercises at home and you make a mistake at a show you can come home and go through familiar exercises to rebuild his confidence.

Show Jumping Competitions

SHOW JUMPING can be divided into four levels of competition:

1. Unaffiliated show jumping.
2. Affiliated show jumping at Novice level.
3. Affiliated show jumping at Intermediate level.
4. Show jumping at Grand Prix and International level.

Unaffiliated or unrecognised show jumping competitions

Horses and riders jumping in this category of competition don't have to be registered with any governing body, nor do the organisers or the officials. The competitions do not necessarily adhere to any particular rules and there are no limiting heights of fences. One big drawback to this section of the sport is that as there is no governing body there are no official judging or course building standards. These competitions also attract pot-hunters – people on older, more experienced horses who have no particular aims or ambitions other than to win trophies and ribbons and the limited amount of prize money offered at such competitions.

For the more dedicated show jumper these shows still have their uses though. They can be used to produce a fairly calm, sensible horse who is ready to step up to affiliated shows. They are also a good place for novice riders to start honing their skills before moving on to greater things. Finally, unaffiliated competitions will allow you to gauge whether or not your horse has got what it takes to become a show jumper before you invest in registration, and also for you to decide whether show jumping is for you or not.

A young horse at his first show will be spooky and nervous. He needs a confident and secure rider to help him over his 'first night nerves'.

Many venues which stage affiliated shows will also run one or two unaffiliated competitions before they run their affiliated classes. Try to take your horse to these venues because you know that the fences used and the course built will be up to a recognised standard. A show jumping course built by a person who is not aware of the technical intricacies of course design is likely to damage your horse's confidence rather than build it, as he tries to make impossible distances and unreasonable turns.

Novice show jumping under affiliated or recognised rules

To break into the wonderful world of affiliated show jumping takes motivation and determination. Lying in your bed you may dream you can win any number of show jumping competitions; you can climb Everest in a day and you can glide effortlessly down the black ski runs. When reality bites things are a bit different and, from the top of that slippery slope, things can look a bit trickier! However, you can be brave and take the plunge, starting off down the black run and doing the best you can, or you can put your tail between your legs and slink off home, never knowing what might have been.

To anybody who has an ambition to show jump and thinks they have the ability and determination needed to do it well, my only words of advice are, go ahead and do it properly – register with your country's governing association – in Great Britain it's British Showjumping (BS). Once you have done so you will never look back and hopefully, never regret it. The much-enhanced courses will certainly improve you and your horse and the stiffer competition should make you try harder. You will also want to seek training to improve both yourself and your horse

as, no doubt, once you have stepped up into that bigger, more competitive world then you will want to win.

It is a very big step up, if not physically, then at least mentally. Jumping under BS rules means you are going to be riding against some professional riders at shows held at major venues. The courses you are going to jump may not be bigger than the ones you have been jumping at local shows, but they will appear to be. A well-built BS course (or that of any recognised federation) will be full of colour, use lots of good poles and fillers and will invariably look more imposing than those of the unrecognised shows you are used to.

In general, the whole set-up at an affiliated show will be safer and more professional than at your local show. The access and parking spaces will be more acceptable; the riding surface should be even and, on the whole, better prepared. The courses will all be built by an approved panel course builder and official

Above left: A suitable partnership can take years to form and the right horse years to find, but when it works it will give you endless fun.

Above right: A horse jumping at the top of his game is poetry in motion.

Age classes are a valuable stepping stone for the young horse.

judges, well versed in the rules and in safety procedures, will oversee the entire event.

Shows recognised by the BS offer a wide range of competitions for every grade of horse. At the starting level there are now Intro. classes with fences as low as 0.7m (approx 2ft 3in). Classes then rise progressively in height right through to International Trials which are 1.55m (approx. 5ft).

The height of fences used in the first round of the Novice and Preliminary classes must not exceed 0.90m (3ft). The course will include two double combinations but will not have a treble or a water jump – although there is some discretion allowed by the judge or course builder. At the second round of a Novice Qualifier the fences will be up to 1m (3ft 3in) and again, although there are two double combinations, there will be no treble or water jump. In the Junior Preliminary classes the fences will be up to 0.85m (approx. 2ft 9in) in the first round and up to 1m (3ft 3in) in the second round. For the Seniors the speed is set at 325m per minute and, in Junior competitions, it is 300m per minute. There will be a time allowed (over which time penalties will added) and a time limit (exceeding which incurs elimination) in all recognised or affiliated competitions; these times are based on the set speed at which the horse is required to travel.

The height of fences used in the first round of Senior Newcomers Preliminary classes will not exceed 1.10m (3ft 7in). In these classes you will come up against your first treble combination and may be asked to jump a water tray. A small water jump, not exceeding 2.50m (8ft 2in), may be included, as long as there is a straightforward alternative fence. The biggest increase in height from the first round competition to the second round competition is in the Senior Newcomers as it goes up to 1.25m (4ft 2in) in the first round of the second round competition. (The dual use of 'round' here may seem confusing, but it reflects current use by organising bodies such as British Showjumping. To clarify the point, the height difference mentioned is not between one round and another on the same day, but between 'rounds' of a competition that progresses over a period of time in discrete stages.)

In Junior Newcomers Preliminary classes you will not be expected to jump a treble combination or a water jump. The fences will not exceed 1m (3ft 3in) and, in the second round (see above), 1.15m (3ft 9in). Again the speed set for the Seniors is 325m per minute and for Juniors 300m per minute.

The jump-off course in any class will be raised by a minimum of 5cm (2in) and at least two fences will be raised by a maximum of 10cm (4in). Fences in combinations may not necessarily be raised at all.

Other classes such as the Foxhunter series and Grade C competitions are still considered 'Novice' classes, but they do ask some more questions for the true amateur and are really better described as 'Intermediate' classes. For those less experienced riders, who have obtained a schoolmaster on whom to learn their trade, the BS Member's Cup is an invaluable competition. It allows riders who are not in the top 200 on the national computer rankings to compete on horses of any grade. In the first round of this competition the fences will not exceed 1.15m (3ft 9in). Many shows also host amateur-owner competitions which allow like-minded people to compete among themselves.

Every country will have their own equivalent to these classes and the rules are usually similar. This category could be considered the 'make or break' stage, where you can make the big decision to 'step up' to the Intermediate levels, or decide that you are comfortable where you are.

Affiliated or recognised jumping at Intermediate level

By the time you are jumping courses of 1.20m (4ft) and above, in classes such as Foxhunter, National Grade C and perhaps even National Grade B classes, you are jumping more seriously challenging courses. All of these courses will include a treble combination and may include water trays and water jumps. These competitions are the ultimate aim of many riders and they are contested by serious, talented amateurs, rubbing shoulders with the top riders bringing on their future stars. This level of competition is not impossible to compete at as an amateur rider, but it is a lot more difficult for the amateur to win at.

Even the top shows have classes for up-and-coming young horses in their International arenas.

Young Riders (ages 16–21), competing in this range of competition, will be expected to jump anything up to 1.45m (4ft 9in) and Juniors, up to age 16, will be expected to jump courses of approximately 1.30m (4ft 3in).

The speed that you will be required to travel at in these competitions, will range from 350m per minute in the Foxhunter and Grade C competitions to 375–400m per minute in the Grade B competitions, so you will gradually have to learn to increase your horse's tempo and to walk courses carefully, finding places to shave off valuable metres.

Jumping at International level

This is it; the ultimate challenge. Competitions at this level include International competitions and International trials. The fences in the first rounds of these competitions may be up to 1.60m (5ft 3in). Most proficient riders will ultimately feel comfortable jumping at up to 1.30m (4ft 3in), but many will start to struggle above that height. To break into the top echelons of any sport is hard but this should not put talented people off. If we did not have young, dedicated and ambitious riders chipping away at the big players, then the sport would soon die.

Below left: I think this guy wants to win.

Below right: Is it home time yet?

Skill, financial support, an ability to stay calm under pressure, an indomitable, insatiable desire to win and an unshakable belief in your own ability as a rider, are all-important at this standard. That's why riders who compete at this level are totally self-motivated and doggedly self-disciplined. If you fit that description then the sky is your limit.

Before the Show

The importance of pre-show checks

BEFORE YOU EVEN THINK ABOUT GOING TO A SHOW, you need to go through the following checklist and be able to say 'yes' to everything. Is your horse obedient to your aids? Are you fit? Is he fit? How long has he been in work? Are you feeding good quality food appropriate to the work he is doing? Is he fat and flabby or sleek and well muscled? Are his teeth, feet and back in a healthy state? Is he fully sound, with no hint of encroaching spavin or splint? Is he totally free of virus, cough or runny nose? Is his worming and vaccination regime up to date? Do your saddle and bridle, including the bit, fit correctly and are they safe? Are they clean? Is all your auxiliary equipment (brushing boots, rugs, headcollars, etc.) clean and safe? Is your horse too fresh? A really fresh horse is not likely to perform at his best, as he will be too fizzy to do so.

If you can say 'Yes' to everything, then you need have no worries about taking your horse to a show because he is in good health and ready for action. The point that I am trying to make is that horses do not become nappy and bad-tempered just because they want to; it is nearly always because they have been pushed beyond their capabilities or have been asked to do something when they are not fit to do it. Horses and riders only have the basic talent, mentally and physically, that they are born with. If you recognise and accept these limitations, it is almost guaranteed that you will make progress.

The biggest mistake you can make on the morning of a show is to get up late and rush around. Do you remember the last time you left everything to the last minute when you went on holiday and the panic that you felt running to the check-in? Well, the panic that your horse feels as you run about getting in a flap is greater because he has no idea why you are doing so. If you are lucky enough to have a brilliant groom, you may be able to stay in bed until all the work's done, but nobody that I ever worked for did that; they were too concerned for the welfare of their horses.

Planning prevents panic

The plan you make should suit you at every show that you go to, provided that it is a sound plan to begin with. I know that plans don't always work, but if you don't have one you will not necessarily know that something is missing or wrong. Every good rider learns to adopt a system. They know from experience that it works, and so they always attempt to do things in the same order.

Try to work out, on paper, at what time you need to leave. Work backwards from the start of the class. Give yourself 30 minutes to warm up and to be ready, standing at the side of the collecting ring steward, when your number is called. Take into account learning and walking the course, preparing yourself, getting tacked up, (including the removal of all travelling gear and putting on of all boots and equipment), collecting your numbers, unloading your horse, organising your crew and acquainting yourself with the showground lay out, including finding the ring in which you are going to jump!

Also, think about how long it is going to take you to get to the showground, allowing time for traffic hold-ups and getting lost. At home, think about how long it is going to take you to carry out your normal stable routine, plus prepare yourself, your horse and his equipment and load up the lorry. Try to get as much done as possible the day before the show and give yourself an extra 30 minutes at the end of your timetable to allow for hitches. Try to err on the generous side with your timings; things always seem to take longer than you think they will, especially if you are riding a young horse who has now turned into an uncaged lion and you are so nervous that you are all fingers and thumbs!

Have three separate lists of things you need to take:

- One for your horse.
- One for you.
- One for your lorry.

Tick items off as they are put in the lorry. As you go to more and more shows you will become more naturally organised and less dependent on your lists. One day you may not even need a written list, but take heed, there is nothing more galling than putting in all the hard work necessary to get to a show, only to find out that you can't compete because you have forgotten your riding hat. I have, over the years, forgotten everything it is possible to forget, including the horse!

Of course, in time, you will be more relaxed about everything, but training for everything connected with show jumping requires planning and good practice.

Getting There

Travelling safely

BEFORE YOU LOAD YOUR HORSE, you must ensure that he is well protected against the rigours of travelling. Whether you use specially designed protective travelling boots or bandages is up to you. Travelling boots will protect the horse from damage but provide little support, whereas stable bandages provide support but little protection. The best way to provide both support and protection is to use leg wraps and stable bandages. Tails should be protected both by tail bandages and tail guards attached to the roller and tail bandages. (However, there are now tail guards that don't need a roller to hold them in place and these are my preference.) Remember to tie your tail bandage below the dock – it has been known for a horse's tail to actually fall off through tying a knot too tight around the dock, cutting off circulation – so beware!

Remember that if your lorry is well ventilated, it is a good idea to travel the horse in a warm rug in the winter. Modern thermal rugs are excellent. They are warm and wick the horse's moisture from his body to the outside of the rug. During the winter I might put a woollen day rug over the thermal rug, once the horse has arrived at the show and is standing around. If it is an exceptionally hot day use a light rug or no rug at all, but you will still need to use a roller for a traditional tail guard. Poll guards are a sensible precaution if you are travelling in a trailer, but are less essential if you are travelling in a purpose-built lorry.

To guarantee that your horse arrives at the show in a relaxed state, make sure that his journey is as stress-free as possible. If your horse travels badly he will lose weight and condition as he sweats up. He will become stressed and tense, leading to panic and injury. You do not need a £250,000 pantechnicon with Jacuzzi, sauna, satellite TV and air conditioning to travel your horse in safety and comfort, but you do need a reliable, well-ventilated lorry or trailer which is in good condition.

There used to be a great fuss made that, when travelling, the horse must face

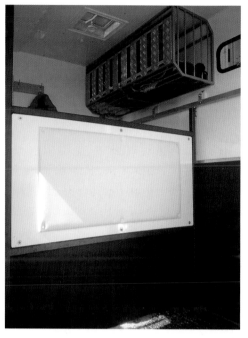

A good workmanlike horsebox. Light and airy, with sensible flooring, padded partitions, storage for feed and tack and a safe, shallow ramp. Any horse will arrive at a show in a good state of mind having travelled in comfort.

away from the engine, so that if the brakes had to be applied suddenly, the horse would sit on his bottom, rather than lunge forward. My opinion is that a horse will get used to travelling in any direction, as long as he feels safe and has enough room to spread his legs if he needs to.

Ensure that the footing in your lorry or trailer is safe, including that on the ramp. Rubber matting is an ideal, slip-free surface but shavings encourage the horse to relieve himself if he needs to, so a reasonable layer of shavings underneath the horse will provide him with some comfort. Do have your lorry or trailer serviced regularly – this includes renewing wooden floorboards when appropriate. A horse falling through the floor when travelling is obviously an extremely traumatic and dangerous experience, not only for the horse but also for the driver and the driver of the car behind! Yes – it has happened.

Tie your horses short enough that they cannot fight or get their heads over, or under, partitions. Make sure that each horse has enough space and adequate ventilation. Drive sympathetically by driving slowly through bends and do not slam on the brakes as you hurtle towards a roundabout, but slow down gradually through the gears. If you are undergoing a long journey, of eight hours or more, you should allow your horse rest time in which he can stretch his legs, have a small drink and perhaps a small feed. Whether or not your horse has a haynet whilst he travels is up to you. Personally I feel that horses go to shows to perform as athletes and that they are less likely to be able to do so if they have a belly full of hay.

When you arrive

When you arrive at the showground, if you have the time, walk your horse around for a few minutes to stretch his legs, nibble a blade of grass or two, relax and possibly urinate. Horses don't like to urinate in an enclosed space and they will perform better if they have an empty bladder.

At a show you will face many new challenges, more negatively known as problems! The first half an hour, especially for the young horse and/or novice rider, is always the worst. First, both you and your horse are going to be excited; you will be thinking about everything other than the work plan that you had made so carefully at home the previous night and your horse will be looking everywhere, other than where he is meant to be going. Your first show will always be the worst, as far as nerves go, because your horse is going to be totally overawed by all the other horses, the flags flying, the bright colours and the public address system.

One of the reasons why I have said, many times before, that you must 'wake up the dragon' at home and ride your horse to a much higher level there, is to enable you to have a cushion, once you get to your first show. If the height and technicality of the fences at the show are less than those you have been practising over at home, then that is one less thing for you to worry about.

Taking along a helper or coach

Make sure that you take the right helper as, if the person you are with is nagging you and telling you to 'do this' or 'do that' and isn't letting you ride with your own natural flair, that suppression is going to have a negative effect on the way

POINTS TO PONDER...

> If you think you can, you can; if you think you can't, then you can't, then you're right.

that you do things. Your natural flair has to be directed. The excitement and adrenalin buzz of being at a show will only improve your performance as long as you can control these feelings *positively*. It is too easy to have inappropriate or negative thoughts put into your head if you suppress your own feelings. If the person with you is not sufficiently receptive to your opinions then their inappropriate opinions and deeds may manifest themselves in the arena. Your adviser must not argue with you about what's gone wrong or, worse still, about something that may go wrong. If you argue about things that only *may* go wrong, then something almost certainly *will* go wrong!

If you take your coach with you, then their job is to encourage you and promote feelings of confidence and security in your mind before the performance. After the performance the trainer's job is to systematically analyse and discuss your effort, not to destroy your ego in one fell swoop. It is important that you and your coach dwell on the positives, discussing questions such as: 'What did you like about your round and what would you like to improve in the next round?' These are more important than hearing: 'What the hell did you think you were doing?' or, even worse: 'That was rubbish.' Riders do actually know when they ride badly and, when they make mistakes, they don't need to be told.

It is your job, once you are in the arena, to do your own thing. Right or wrong, good or bad, that is what you have to do. Certainly an inquest may be necessary, but it must be short, to the point and constructive. If the person you are with thinks about what is going on inside your head intelligently, they can be a boon, not a curse. Train to perfection at home – and in the ring, ride instinctively. This does not mean that you throw all your training and practice out of the window as soon as the bell goes but, hopefully, if you have trained and practised sufficiently at home, you will be able to think and ride *instinctively*, if things start to go pear-shaped in the ring.

Eliminating pressure

Pressure to do well is likely to change your riding style and not always for the better. This pressure may come from many different directions but two in particular are an *internal* pressure to do well and an *external* pressure to please other people. The pressure to do well, as far as your own ambition is concerned, can be coped with quite easily but, when the pressure to do well is coming from friends, owners, trainers, sponsors, father, mother, grandparents and the family dog, then it can start to get to you. If those pressures are not kept under control then they will directly affect your horse, as your anxieties are transmitted to him and things will start to go wrong.

One of the best ways to start eliminating pressure is not to go to a show until you know you are ready – in fact you need to be more ready than you think you are! There is no point in going to a show on a wing and a prayer, but this doesn't mean that you can't go to a small schooling show to find out where your weaknesses lie, as we have already discussed.

Another important way of eliminating pressure is to make sure that you are not going to overstretch yourself, by jumping in at the deep end and entering a class that is too big for you and your horse's present ability, or experience. It is lovely to buy an experienced horse who is jumping well around 1.35m (4ft 6in) courses and to take him into 1.10m (3 ft 7in) classes, to gain experience and confidence. But if you are riding an inexperienced horse and you are trying to create confidence, you must remember that confidence takes months to build and seconds to destroy. Only a few mistakes will not only destroy your horse's confidence but also your faith in yourself. As I have mentioned before, although you must have an ultimate goal – be it competing in the Olympics or in an Open class at a local show – you must also have a goal which is achievable, within the foreseeable future. Never make your short- or long-term goals totally unobtainable; they must be realistic if you and your horse are to progress smoothly.

Pressure and young, green horses

When they are young and green, I will sometimes take my horses to a local unaffiliated show, where there are no great expectations. The jumps are bland and there is no great excitement going on. The stress put on young horses, when travelling them to their first few shows, is often not taken seriously enough. Horses, like us, do feel stress. This stress may manifest itself in different ways, the most obvious being for the horse to break out in a sweat. How often do you see the ramp come down at a show and steam escaping from the lorry as if from a Turkish bath!

I will trot a youngster around a 0.6m (2ft) course so that I can assess how he is likely to react at larger shows, later in his career. It is quite important to find out what your horse's reaction is likely to be at a show because it gives more insight into his psyche than you will ever have at home. Do not expect to jump a round of show jumps on your first visit to a show. If your horse is too excited, just let him soak up the atmosphere, become calm and then take him home. The old saying: 'All your geese are swans at home', is never as true as when, on arriving at a show, you find that your beautiful swan is rapidly turning into an ugly duckling!

CHAPTER 17

Walking the Course

WALKING THE COURSE is as important as riding it. Put away your mobile phone, stop the social chatter and concentrate. Your first view of the course is the view your horse will get, so remember what you thought when you saw the big, scary oxer, or the tricky turn. If you walk the course with your coach don't be afraid to ask questions and do listen to the coach's advice, that's what they are there for.

It is not enough just to know in what direction you have to jump the course, or in what order the fences come. You must walk the course thoroughly and methodically but, before you even set foot in the arena, you must study the course plan to have a basic idea of where you are going. Note the position of the entrance,

The first view of the ring can sometimes be intimidating.

the start and the finish, as well as the speed required and time allowed for each round. Obviously you don't want to hurtle around the course but neither do you wish to incur time faults. If you see that the course is to be ridden at 350m per minute, then you know that you will have to ride a little more quickly than if the speed required were 325m per minute. You will, therefore, have to slightly increase your speed and/or have to ride your corners a little tighter.

Once you know where you are going on paper, you can begin to walk the course. The view you get walking it for the first time gives you an idea of the first view *your* horse is going to get. Once again, please remember, that if the view you get is frightening, then you can be sure that your horse is going to find it frightening too! If you round a corner and come face to face with a huge yellow and black oxer with massive fillers with black holes in them and think: 'Oh help, look at that!' you can bet your bottom dollar that your horse will think exactly the same. As you walk up to the fence you must think about how you are going to approach it and *be sure of this*, before you get on your horse.

POINTS TO PONDER... Remember make a plan. Plans don't always work, but if you don't have one it can't work.

Fence by fence

Hopefully the first fence will be an inviting one that will encourage you to ride towards it, without fear of knocking it down easily. Occasionally you will come across course builders who will build an upright, or a very square fence, as a first fence – not very friendly – especially on a Novice course, but it still has to be jumped. More usually, the first fence will be an ascending oxer, or a small triple bar. A cross-bar spread, which is well filled in with a brush, is a good first fence as it encourages your horse to focus his attention on the job in hand and jump well. If your horse jumps the first fence well, it will give you boundless confidence to jump the following ones well.

Next walk from the first fence to the second fence. Remember your yard-long paces (as discussed in Chapter 11). Four of these paces are equal to one of your horse's strides. Allow two yards (two paces), from behind the base of the first fence, to be where your horse will land, and two yards (two paces), from in front of the second fence, to be where your horse will take off from. Thus one of your groups of four paces, from one fence to the next, is taken up by landing and taking off. The remainder of your groups of four paces represent the horse's strides between the two fences.

What kind of fence is the second fence? Is the distance between it and the first fence related? Is it directly in front of the first fence, or do you have to turn a corner to get to it? If the distance is on a curved line, walk the distance between the two fences as if you were riding it – take the same route as you intend to take on your horse. Once you have arrived at the second fence, turn back and see where you have come from. How has the striding worked out through your curve? If the striding seems odd, go back and walk your line again. If the striding still seems odd, consider whether you ought to slightly widen or narrow your line between the two, thus making the strides your horse will take more regular, or whether you ought, in fact, to hold him on a shortened stride, to get through the curve. Keep walking the line you want to take until you are quite clear in your mind where and how you are going to ride it.

In the modern-day sport it is essential to walk all of the distances even through the turns. Every distance should be ridden as is set. If you are going to aspire to ride at a high level it is important to start off as you mean to go on, which means teaching yourself to ride at the correct speed and on the correct number of strides through the set distance. It is only necessary to use your initiative on those occasions when things do not go according to plan.

Think about all of these things as you progress around the course. At each combination or related distance remember that eight paces (yards) between two fences is equal to one non-jumping stride; 12 paces (yards) is equal to two non-jumping strides; 16 paces (yards) is equal to three non-jumping strides, etc. Distances between fences can be lengthened or shortened at the whim of the course builder, so as you walk the course, try to assess how the course builder intends to see the course jumped. Is the distance between the double 13 paces (if so, the course builder would like to see your horse moving on an open stride), or is it 11 paces (in which case the course builder would like to see your horse moving on a short, bouncy stride)?

Divide the course into all the exercises you have been practising at home: straight line related distances, curved line related distances, single and double fences. This will take the mystery and fear out of the competition course and reduce it to those familiar tasks that you have been setting yourself at home, on a regular basis, for weeks. Walk each exercise separately, using your corners to link them together and then walk the course as a whole, still mentally dividing it into your separate sections.

You must also keep in your mind's eye an idea of how you are going to approach each fence. Is your horse likely to spook at any of the fences? In this case you are going to have to ride him into those fences quite strongly. Perhaps he is more likely to run at some of them? If this is the case then you are going to have to keep him on a short, bouncy stride. Think about where each fence is, in relation to the exit and the other horses. Most horses will jump more freely if jumping towards 'home', but they may not be so careful. Some horses can be a little nappy when jumping away from 'home' – not keen to leave their friends behind – so make sure that you walk the course with your horse's character in mind.

Each time you come to a fence, study what type it is. Is it an oxer, a vertical, a hog's back or a triple bar? What kind of oxer is it: a square or an ascending oxer?

All competitors walk the course in their own way, but it is a serious business.

What kind of combination are you being asked to jump; does it consist of two uprights or is it an upright to an oxer?

You must study the turns and the distances and note the position of the start and finish. There is nothing more galling than being eliminated for not going through the start or finish and it is no good coming to a halt as soon as you have landed over the final fence, accruing time faults for not having gone through the finish.

Visualising the whole

So, you have walked the course and know exactly where you are going and how you are going to ride to each fence. The course is well planned in your head. Now sit down quietly, shut your eyes and ride the course in your head a couple of times, jumping a beautifully judged clear round. See yourself riding the course, either as you would on a video, or as you would if you were on your horse's back, seeing each fence approach between your horse's ears. See and feel what problems could occur and how you would deal with them. Familiarise yourself with every eventuality but especially that beautifully ridden and timed clear round – convince yourself that this is the round you are going to achieve – there is great merit in positive visualisation.

Help and advice from a more experienced rider is often invaluable.

Riding In – Collecting Ring Technique

NOW IT IS TIME TO GET ON YOUR HORSE and prepare him for his round. When you are warming up your horse, the effect you're trying to achieve is a state of complete tranquillity and harmony between you. You are trying to produce a quietly submissive, supple horse in balance, in rhythm and one who is active and mentally alert. Your sound proficiency is going to eliminate tension and inconsistency! Unfortunately, this is not always possible, as other riders and their horses suddenly cut across your track, taking no notice of the flagging: they jump fences backwards, cannoning into your horse's quarters and running out just in front of you.

Once you are in the warm-up area, your horse has to work to warm up properly. Don't slop along for hours on a long rein, talking to your friends, then thrash him around at the last moment, throwing him over half a dozen big fences, before dashing into the arena. You must concentrate on working your horse in such a way that, when he starts jumping fences, he is going to jump them well. This may take a little while but if your horse is not paying you any attention when you warm up then you are going to crash and burn when you attempt to jump him.

The practice jump area is a warming-up area – it is not a schooling ground. By the time you have arrived at the showground your horse should be prepared to jump anything within his scope and should not need to jump the practice fence endlessly, in order to make him (or you) better or braver.

Work your horse quietly on the flat and have him level, both physically and mentally before you jump the practice fence. Once you are ready to jump, start with a small cross-pole or vertical just to loosen him up a bit and then raise the fence steadily. I feel that within half a dozen jumps you should have reached the height that you will be jumping in the arena. Then you can jump over an oxer; once again start quite low to make sure that your horse gets the idea that nothing is going to frighten him, but you can build the oxer up more rapidly. However, make sure that it is neither too big nor too wide – you are not trying to test your

horse, or school him in the collecting ring, but simply asking him to stretch and open out a little. Finally, give yourself a little time to walk around, before jumping another vertical which may be *slightly* higher than you will jump in the arena.

So many times you see riders jumping over and over again in the collecting ring. The only thing I can put this down to is that their schooling at home has not been thorough enough and they are still trying to get things right now. What is even worse is the rider who seems to practise getting things wrong by trying to jump too high or wide and continually having refusals. I can only put this down to bad coaching, lack of confidence or plain stupidity.

Make sure that you arrive at the entrance to the arena in good time for your round. There is nothing more disconcerting, for you or your horse, than to be hustled into the arena by an irate collecting steward, who has been calling your name for five minutes – nor anything more annoying for your fellow competitors, than to be held up by your incompetence. On the other hand, don't sit in the entrance on your horse, to watch six or seven horses before you. Watching other people's rounds is a good idea but do it on your own, on foot, so that you aren't getting in the way of everybody else, whilst your horse starts to get cold and stiff after warming up.

Ideally it is only necessary to start jumping, during your warm-up, when there are about five or six horses before you. This will give you time to 'jump in', make sure you are comfortable and give your horse time to catch his breath, before entering the arena.

A few words on collecting ring etiquette. Bad manners in riders and helpers at the practice fence are, unfortunately, all too common. There are riders who think they have the right to lay claim to the practice fence, for as long as they wish, regardless of others. Such hogging of the fence is the most irritating habit. Cutting

Above left and middle: The important thing is to ride-in quietly and in a relaxed manner.

Above right: Some work to supple up, such as shoulder-in, is a great help before you start to jump.

A watchful eye is invaluable.

in and altering the fence, when another rider is in mid warm-up, is another. Being cut up by someone in a hurry to get to the fence is not only irritating but dangerous. The habit of jumping 30cm (1ft) higher than the biggest fence on the course not only delays everyone else's warm-up, but is totally unnecessary. At the top end of show jumping there is an unwritten rule that everyone waits their turn and respects the other riders and horses. Unfortunately, as you filter down the ranks, good manners, through ignorance of proper practice, get thinner. Good coaches should teach their young riders correct etiquette from an early age.

It is a great confidence-builder when the horse feels good in the warm-up.

The First Round

THERE ARE MANY DIFFERENT TYPES OF COMPETITION in modern-day show jumping. BS has introduced some time-saving initiatives to help riders, especially if a rider has two or three horses in the same competition. The Single Phase is a class where, no matter how many fences you have down in the first part of the round, you may proceed immediately to the jump-off. A Two Phase is a little different in that, if you have a fence down in the first section, then the bell will sound and you must leave the ring. All of the new rules will, of course, be found in the BS Rule Book. (The show jumping associations of other countries may have similar classes.) The precise nature of the class in which you will be jumping will, of course, be a factor in how you plan to ride your first round.

Once you are in the arena, remember the plans you have made in your head. Get your horse into a balanced, rhythmic canter, leading with the correct leg for your first turn and remember to ride though the start. Remember that the course is not one huge, daunting bowl of spaghetti. Ride to each exercise as you have planned, using all your corners. This will give you more time to think about each fence. Once you have gone through the finish get into the habit of making a circle, getting your horse under control and working well, almost as if you are going to start again. Do not get into the dreadful habit of flying out of the ring or dragging your horse into a sliding halt. Finally if, during your round, you have a pole down – *forget about it* – you cannot put it back up. Neither can you concentrate on the fences ahead of you, if you are trying to analyse what went wrong at the fences behind you.

Once you have jumped your round, for better or worse, do not make a scene. Hopefully you have jumped a good clear that you feel comfortable with but, if you have not, just get straight off once you are out of the arena and keep calm. There is absolutely no need for some of the horrible 'spoilt brat' scenes that you occasionally see in collecting rings (or, even more inexplicably, back in the horsebox area or stables) at some of the smaller shows; young or, worse still, not

The first round should be as unhurried and unruffled as possible, giving the horse and rider confidence.

POINTS TO PONDER...

Bad
tempers
don't win
arguments.

so young people, taking their anger out on their poor horses – raking spurs, pulling out back teeth or unnecessary abuse of the whip. Nor is there any need for you to scream at your parents, friends or trainer. What has been done is done. Learn from your mistakes and go home and iron your problems out there, in a civilised manner. If you can not control your temper, get off and walk away.

Whatever the form of competition, after you leave the ring, you should trot the horse on a long rein for a few minutes to break down the build-up of any lactic acid in the muscles, then walk him until his breathing is back to normal. Loosen the girth and either you, or your helper, should walk him around for another five or ten minutes with a warm rug or a cooler, depending on the weather.

In this picture a young horse in his early career looks very secure in the first round of competition.

This rider looks very happy in what may well be this young horse's first venture into the International arena as a six-year-old.

The Jump-Off

Defining your aims

FIRST YOU MUST DEFINE YOUR AIMS IN THE JUMP-OFF. Are you trying to win the competition, or are you trying to gain experience? If you are trying to gain experience, you should focus on raising the level of activity in your horse and raising your own concentration. Study the course on the course plan before you look at the jumps in the arena. Look for some sensible short turns to encourage you both to move up a gear. There is little point in wandering around aimlessly, jumping fences for the sake of it. You should be practising quietly and sensibly, with future wins as your goal. Make calculated turns, so that your horse is used to being turned in short to fences and increase your tempo a little, so that he becomes accustomed to being ridden in a slightly up-tempo rhythm.

If you are trying to win the competition, you need to study the course in even greater detail to analyse all the possible options where tight turns can be risked and strides lengthened. Try to have an edge over the other competitors. Look for something that no one else is likely to see and take that risk. The great thing about show jumping is that if you try and it comes off, you are today's hero; if you fail you may look a bit of a fool, but so what – at least you tried! Once again, study the course first on the written plan and then study the course and fences in the arena. Make sure you have studied:

- All the short turns.
- Where you can lengthen.
- Where you need to shorten.
- How each fence, jumped in a certain way, can lead you on well to the next one.
- Whether you can angle a jump over one fence (see later this chapter) to get inside another.
- Where the start and finish are.

CHAPTER 20

Riding in a jump-off is all about riding wisely, with daring, but not recklessly. Remember, again, if you are quick-thinking you will have more time to act. Whether you are jumping to gain experience or to win, you will need to pick up your jump-off tempo before you go through the start. If trying to win, do not harbour any doubts or reservations – try to win from the first stride to the last.

Jump-off techniques

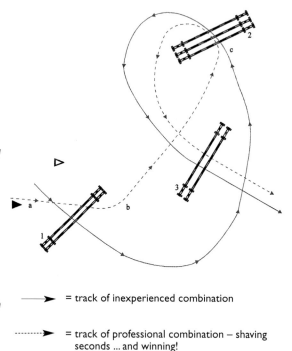

Jump-off technique.

(a) Coming close to the offside start flag allows the horse to jump the first fence at an angle.

(b) Turning on landing, towards the second fence, allows the horse to cut inside the third fence.

(c) Turning the horse in the air over the second fence allows for a sharp turn to the third fence.

It is easy to see how time and distance can be saved but unless your horse is balanced and well schooled he will be unable to perform such turns. If your horse is stiff and resistant, attempting tight turns will actually waste time as you will be unable to maintain a forward canter stride. You will also run the risk of having refusals, run-outs or knock-downs.

————▶ = track of inexperienced combination

------▶ = track of professional combination – shaving seconds ... and winning!

Once you are ready to attack jump-off courses with the intention of winning the class, you need to know how to do so; how to turn into fences quickly and from a short distance; how to turn sharply after fences; how to jump across fences on an angle and how to turn up the tempo.

Turning short into fences

The essential ingredient for turning short into fences is to be confident and positive about doing so. Primarily, you need to practise at home, time and time again. To turn short into your fences you need very good balance and a bold attitude. To practise at home, set up a small fence and jump it through a circle. Gradually reduce the size of your circle from approximately 20m to 15m, then to 10m. Always keep your horse balanced between strong hand and leg aids and encourage him to produce the strong, rhythmic canter which is one gear up from the speed at which you would normally ride. The outside leg and rein are really important in the tight turn and 'popping out' through the shoulders or quarters will mess up the turn and lose impulsion. Eventually your horse will become accustomed to meeting the fence off a curve from a short distance and to reacting quickly.

Next, you can increase the height of the fence and begin to put obstacles in the way of your approach. For instance, you can place a fence wing a few metres in front of the fence and you will aim to turn inside the wing. Immovable objects, around which you will have to manoeuvre your horse, are a feature of the competition jump-off and your ability to move fluently inside these obstacles, taking the shortest route from fence to fence, will ultimately affect whether you win a class or become an also-ran.

Never look at the fence or obstacle that you are trying to avoid. Once you commit yourself to a turn you must not take your eye off the fence you are about to jump, until you are jumping it. If you do take your eye off the fence you are aiming for, you will either over- or undershoot it: your eye will be drawn to something that you are trying to avoid. If you are looking at something you are trying to avoid, the chances are that you will ride straight into it! Conversely, if you are trying to ride though a gap – look through the gap.

Once you have committed yourself to a turn, don't change your mind. Occasionally, when you have turned the corner and are approaching the fence, you will find yourself in a less-than-perfect take-off spot – don't panic. If you are too far away, keep hold of your horse's head and use plenty of leg. If you have found yourself too close to the fence, again just take a stronger hold on the reins and encourage your horse to create a higher jump. Always ride with a good amount of leg, indicating to your horse: 'Yes, we are going and don't worry about a thing.' If you attempt to alter the shape of your curve as you approach the fence, you will unbalance your horse and he will come to the base of the fence in a disorganised heap.

Another useful exercise is to construct a right angle, with two poles in front of the jump, slightly to one side. Put a cone a couple of metres in from the poles and ride your horse between the cones and the poles as you turn into the jump. This will help to improve your balance on the approach to a fence.

One important lesson to learn is how important the outside leg and rein are, when executing short turns. Any loss of contact with the outside rein will lead to the horse bulging out through the neck and shoulder.

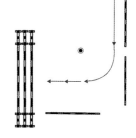

Poles placed like this can help you plan your turn into a fence.

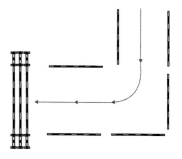

As you practise, you can replace inside poles with a cone so that your turn can be nearer to the fence.

Poles to help guide you through the turn can be very useful in learning jump-off techniques. In this series of pictures we can see the rider concentrating on total control through the turn.

Instigating the turn in the air. To achieve this, riders need to be aware of exactly where they are at all times and to be very calm in the mind so as not to put the horse out of balance. (Note how this rider is in complete harmony and looking precisely where she intends to go.)

To be really good it is essential to practise. This rider is saving valuable time by turning inside a fence to shorten the approach.

Turning short after fences

To practise this, go back to your small single fence on a 20m circle and start to make a change of rein as you jump the fence. As you take off, look to the opposite rein and encourage your horse to land, ready to turn on to the new rein. For example, if you have started your circle on a left bend, look to the right as you take off and turn to the right as you land. Once you have re-established a balanced canter, approach the fence with the intention of turning to the left on landing. Again, look to the left as you take off, to encourage your horse to shift his weight on to his left side and to change lead from right to left.

Next you can begin to make a figure of eight over your fence. Once your horse is happily carrying out this exercise, you can gradually reduce the diameter of your circles to 10m. When you are trying to turn in the air, you not only need to look in the direction in which you intend to turn, but also to make a small adjustment in your weight, through your stirrups, and to guide your horse on to the new rein with a

Using poles and a cone to guide your turn after a fence. As you practise you can get closer and closer to the cone.

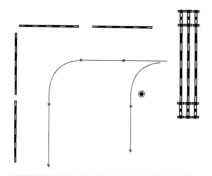

leading rein. Too great an adjustment is more certain to throw your horse off balance than no adjustment at all, so work on subtlety! To refresh your memory on turning, refer back to that heading in Chapter 7.

As a progression from the poles and cone exercise described for turning short into a fence, position a second pair of poles at a right angle, with a central cone after the jump, as well as before it, so you have to perform a balanced turn after you land, as well as before you take off.

Jumping on an angle

Jumping on an angle is part of the ammunition that you need for good jump-off results. The fastest way to get between two points is in a straight line. If you can cut across an angle over a fence with confidence, it can also set you up for a much better turn after the jump. If you are brave enough to ride that straight line, even if an angled fence is in the way, you will beat the rider who makes three or more changes of direction to approach that fence in a straight line.

The most common mistake made by riders coming to a fence at an angle, is to try to turn square to the fence at the very last moment – this shows a lack of confidence. So how do you increase your confidence? Practise at home! To practise jumping on angles you need to give yourself a very clear line to work from. Set up a small upright fence and lay a pole a couple of metres in front of it, at the angle at which you want to jump from. This 'guiding pole' will help you to line you up for the fence. As you become more confident, increase the angle of the pole and eventually, remove it altogether.

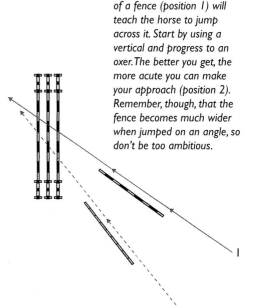

Using an angled pole in front of a fence (position 1) will teach the horse to jump across it. Start by using a vertical and progress to an oxer. The better you get, the more acute you can make your approach (position 2). Remember, though, that the fence becomes much wider when jumped on an angle, so don't be too ambitious.

The most common mistake made by horses coming to fences at an angle, is that they run out through the outside shoulder. You must insure against this eventuality by keeping a firm contact on both reins and a strong outside leg, keeping your horse to the required track. Your priority is to keep your horse channelled between your hands and legs towards the fence and at the point that you want to jump it. The area of the fence that you aim for is exactly the same as if you were approaching it head on – the middle section (metre or so) of the poles or planks. If you keep yourself focused on this area, your horse will be less likely to run out. Jumping fences at an angle will teach you to be more accurate.

Jumping the fence at an angle will shave seconds off your time but requires confidence, concentration and courage. Observe how this rider is putting the horse in no doubt about where they intend to go.

Jumping a figure of eight over a fence at an angle. This is a progression from the exercise shown in the preceding diagram. Try to encourage your horse to land on the correct leg, but if he doesn't, either bring him back to trot and change to the correct lead or perform a flying change.

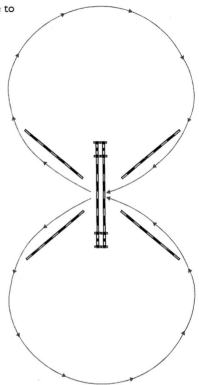

A rider practising angled jumps by riding a figure of eight over the water tray.

Jumping oxers at an angle is more difficult than jumping uprights at an angle. This is because the width of the oxer is naturally greater than an upright to start with, and this width is increased further by jumping it on an angle. You must be careful not to frighten yourself or your horse and you must practise at home before trying to jump an angled oxer in a competition. Build a very small, narrow oxer to start practising over, again using a guiding pole, and gradually increase the height and width of the oxer as you both become more confident and capable.

Once you can jump fences on an angle without using the guide pole, you can jump them through a figure of eight. Put a guide pole a few metres after the fence as well, training you to maintain your line after jumping. It is as important to move away from the fence at the correct angle as it is to approach it from the correct angle. Line up three fences, three or four strides apart, each set at an angle. Use poles to create a channel between the fences and approach the fences from both reins. Progress to jumping double combinations in the same manner, using a staggered or offset double. These exercises will improve your angle jumping, your accuracy and your related distance riding – pretty useful really!

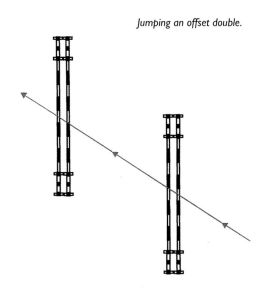

Jumping an offset double.

Throughout all of these exercises you must keep your horse light in his shoulders and powerful in his haunches; you must also enable him to maintain his balance: *balance is the key to saving seconds in the jump-off.*

Remember that you are riding a straight line from Point A to Point B; it is the fence which is at an angle. When you walk a competition course, always keep the jump-off in mind. If you realise that you will want to jump a fence at an angle in the jump-off, walk the angle now. Find yourself a Point A and look towards Point B. Look for a noticeable landmark at Point B, to aim for. From Point B, look back to Point A and check that the line you have drawn for yourself is a good one. Once you are on your horse in the jump-off, as you approach the fence from Point A, keep your eye on that landmark at Point B. This will help you to maintain your straight line and will discourage you from trying to meet the fence straight on.

Upping the tempo

Galloping over show jumps is not the same as galloping over steeplechase fences or fixed obstacles. You cannot brush through or scrape over show jumps; you have to ensure that all the poles are left up. The bigger the fence, the more difficult it is to clear – particularly at the gallop, which produces a long, flat stride. Therefore we do not gallop at fences; we open our horse up over fences and increase his stride after them. Two or three strides before the fence, we return our horse to a rubber-ball canter, so that he is ready to take off in a short, balanced stride.

Try to organise your gallop so that you move on for five or ten strides but are able to close your horse up for three or four strides afterwards. This is something you can practise at home, either in the school or out on a hack. As you close your horse up, think about getting his hocks underneath him, generating energy. This all stems back to our flatwork and creating 'infinite adjustability' within his gaits. You will never win a jump-off if it takes you seven or eight strides to increase or decrease your tempo. Your horse may need some strong hand and leg aids to begin with, to instil in him the idea of instant obedience and tempo change – and the ensuing leaps forward, head-throwing and paddling may not be a very pretty sight. However, the sooner he understands what he is being asked to do, the sooner the aids can be refined. The more you practise, the more responsive your horse will become. Ultimately, your horse will be capable of making quite radical changes to his gait and speed within one or two strides.

POINTS TO PONDER....

Think fast; give yourself more time to act.

The ultimate goal is to achieve a strong, energetic canter with the energy collected between the hands and legs and the kinetic energy working inside the horse's frame and not escaping through the hand or through the shoulders.

This rider is travelling at speed and is clearly in charge, with both horse and rider looking competitive and confident. Note how easily the horse is landing on the right lead, so will easily stay in balance through the turn.

In a much bigger competition the same rules apply. Total concentration under pressure; the rider is already looking to the next fence and the horse will land in balance.

What Happens If…?

CHAPTER 21

THIS CHAPTER LOOKS AT SOME OF THE COMMON PROBLEMS that can confront a rider at a show and offers advice on the best course of action.

MICHEL ROBERT

French Olympic rider, one of the most stylish and accomplished riders in the world.

"Always look for the problem in the mind of the rider, not in the body of the horse. Always look for a solution in the mind of the rider and not in the body of the horse. Take care of the basics and establish them well; overlooking the simple things will always catch up with you and cause difficulties."

What happens if I arrive late?

If you arrive late, for whatever reason (your horse would not load, you got lost, broke down or ran out of diesel) first, do not panic, scream and flap. Panic only ever makes things worse. When you panic you start to rush and when you start to rush, you frighten your horse, forget things, drop things and generally become less effective.

If you do miss the class, well, it is just one class, not the end of civilisation as we know it, but the chances are that if you stay calm, get your horse tacked up, yourself changed and get down to the arena in the quickest time you can, without flustering your horse, you will not miss it. Note the emphasis on not flustering your horse; your horse does not know you are late, so the best thing to do is not to upset him.

Given that you arrive at the collecting ring and there are only a couple of horses left to go in the class or, even worse, they are already calling for you, just canter around the collecting ring for a few minutes, calmly and in good balance, without losing your cool and do not jump the practice fence as a rushed, bad practice jump may cause more harm than good.

You will not have had a chance to walk the course, so you won't be aware of the distances between fences, but you should have seen at least one horse jump the course and, hopefully, someone will have given you some idea of the route. As you enter the arena give the course a quick scan before embarking on your round, but remember that once the bell has gone, you must begin your round within 45 seconds. At most shows the public display clock will count down from 45 seconds. If your horse decides to answer the call of nature during this 45 seconds then you should raise your hand; the judge will stop the clock until he has finished.

Once the bell goes you are no longer late; you are in exactly the same place now as you would be if you had arrived two hours ago, so make the most of it. You must jump your round at exactly the same speed and in exactly the same rhythm that you would have done, if you had had hours of preparation.

Hopefully, the first three fences on a course are not too difficult, so treat those as warm-up fences. Make sure that you ride them as accurately and correctly as you can. Now you have the confidence to start your round at fence four and to jump to the best of your ability.

Had you got in a flap, crashed around a few practice fences, flown into the arena and commenced your round in a state of tense confusion your horse would have become distressed, rigid and totally unbalanced. You would have started jumping in a bad manner, completed a bad round and you can be sure that your day would not have improved!

What if my warm-up goes badly?

You have arrived in plenty of time, you are totally organised, you get to the practice area and… you find the going either bears a resemblance to concrete, or it is hock-deep in mud. Perhaps there are 30 horses cannoning into each other in an area the size of a postage stamp and you cannot give your horse either correct or sufficient warm-up.

To begin with, get out of the warm-up area. Relax and walk around the showground in permitted areas. Compose yourself and try to think of an alternative plan. This is going to involve loosening up your horse as much as you can in walk. You can now use all your 'more advanced flatwork skills' (see Chapter 8) ; shoulder-in, leg-yielding and rein-back exercises are all going to help to loosen your horse in a better way than standing around fretting or trying to dart in and out of a mêlée of other horses.

If there is a lull in the practice arena, you may be able to slip in and carry out a small amount of trot and canter work. However, if the going in the practice area is just impossible to jump out of, you should resort to using the first three fences in the arena as your warm-up jumps (as detailed above), praying that, despite the traffic from other competitors, the going in the arena remains better than that outside it. Remind yourself that your horse is correctly trained and you are jumping within your comfort zone, so you *will* cope.

There are few things worse than trying to warm up in very poor conditions. Each horse in the competition will only jump the fences in the competition once, but they will jump the practice fence six or seven times at least, so imagine how bad the going there is likely to get! Seriously deep and holding ground will not only tire your horse, but will cause him a loss of confidence and may lead to strain and injury of joints, tendons and ligaments.

When you enter the arena, check the going in front of the fences. Most horses will have aimed, correctly of course, for the middle metre of the fence and the ground going towards the centre of the fence is likely to be badly cut up. However, the going a little to either side of the centre, towards the wings, should be much better. Because you are hopefully riding an impeccably schooled horse you can aim him closer to the wings of the fences, without fear of him running out! Obviously there will be other riders in the competition who have read this book so you will not be treading on virgin turf, but you should definitely find better going to either side of the centre of the fences. (This is, of course, only relevant on a grass field showground; on an all-weather surface the going will be standard throughout.)

What if I have done everything right yet I have still jumped a bad round?

This could be anything from having one refusal or a pole down, to skittling poles down left, right and centre, to being eliminated for three refusals or a fall. It could even mean that you have jumped clear but felt that you did not deserve to because you were riding badly (but your horse baled you out) or that you managed to get your horse round despite the fact that he was misbehaving.

Right: This looks really horrendous at first glance. Amazingly, the horse remained on his feet and completed the course.

Below: Almost a disaster but again the rider did not give up and regained his seat.

If your horse jumped clear despite you, put the round behind you, think positively and resolve to do better in the next round. If your horse behaved badly because he was too fresh, work him! After you leave the arena, walk him around for a few minutes to allow him to catch his breath and then, do not jump him over a thousand fences, but work him on the flat. The difficulty is to keep your adrenalin under control and avoid becoming tense because of competition nerves. Walk, trot and canter him, just as you would at home. Give him something to think about, such as frequent transitions, leg-yielding and rein-back. Once you have worked the edge off his freshness, walk him for a little while then let him stand and cool off, before you begin your jumping warm-up for the next class.

If your horse has scattered poles to the four winds, the first thing to remember is to keep your temper under control. You can't turn back the clock and have your round again, so accept defeat graciously. Then analyse *why* you had fences down. Rushed preparation, bad riding, poor warm-up facilities or an over-fresh horse should be easy reasons to pin down but, if none of these was at the root of the problem, you must look deeper. Has your horse got a physical problem? Do not make excuses for him but do trot him up and check whether his gait is normal and whether or not he is totally sound. Does he appear particularly stiff on one rein or another? That could signify muscle problems in his spine. Does he appear 'under the weather' (in which case he may have a virus)? If your horse is suddenly off his feed this is a good sign that something is awry and he may need to have his blood checked by your vet.

Horses can only use their talent if they are fit and well. A long season can jade your horse's enthusiasm and take a toll on his physical and mental well-being and you may have missed subtle changes in his appearance. Stand well back and have a good, detached look at him. Is he lean and fit, or just too thin; conversely, is he well-muscled or just too fat? Is he fit or is he just overfed and fizzy? If you don't feel that you can be objective, ask a knowledgeable friend to assess his condition.

If he doesn't appear to have any glaring physical problems, think about the basics. Has he had good preparation and homework leading up to the event? Is he ready to jump the category of class you have entered? Have you checked his feet, teeth and tack? The list is endless but the important point to make is that horses do not become clumsy because they choose to be; there is nearly always something wrong if they suddenly start having fences down.

Refusals may come about as a result of any of the above problems, but what many riders fail to recognise is that often this problem is of their own making. Perhaps all your preparations have gone to plan and everything appears hunky-dory, apart from one factor – are you overfacing yourself? This does not mean that

A UK legend – winner of almost everything!

JOHN WHITAKER

"The more you practise the better you will be, but you will always be learning from your mistakes. Sit down and think about what you did wrong and try to work out how things could have gone better. Should you have gone faster? Should you have tried to get in one more stride between fences? Once you think you know the answer, store that information and remember to use it when a similar situation arises."

you are chicken or that you doubt your own ability; in fact the whole problem of overfacing yourself may stem from too much bravado and a desire to prove to the world that you are better than you are. For instance, if you have bought a good, experienced horse who has won 1.30m (4ft 3in) classes, your ego may push you to enter classes at this height, when you may only be confident and proficient in 1.10m (3ft 7in) classes. This particular problem is witnessed most often when pony riders are pushed by over-enthusiastic parents, when pony riders make the step up to horses, or when people come to the sport at a mature age and think it all looks rather simple. Sadly very few horses are 'jumping machines'. Confidence, as I have said all along, is fragile; it takes years to build and seconds to shatter. Show jumping is a partnership and even the best horse needs an adequate partner. Imagine putting £1 into the till every time you jump well and taking £5 out every time you jump badly – if you keep overfacing yourself, you will become bankrupt remarkably quickly! Top international riders, jumping 1.60m (5ft 3in) classes, have a wealth of experience and confidence behind them. They are riding horses more than capable of jumping 1.70m (5ft 6in) and at home they will occasionally be asked to do so. These riders are entering the ring knowing that they can call on a wealth of experience and an extra 10cm (4in) of height and scope if they need to. When you buy your schoolmaster, ride him at a height at which you feel confident so that you can call on his extra experience and that little extra height if you need to.

If your horse is really young and you are frightened of spoiling him, the rules are very similar. Try to avoid situations which are likely to invite refusals. Prevention is better than cure. Most horses gain confidence by not being hurt, by doing things well and then receiving praise. This is how a bold, confident horse is produced. If a young horse believes that he will hurt himself once he enters the arena, he will soon start to refuse to jump.

UK Super League rider, former European Champion and three times winner of the Hickstead Derby and winner of the King George V Gold Cup.

PETER CHARLES

Build a partnership in which you and your horse have confidence in each other. Never ask your horse to do something that you are not confident about or that you feel will frighten him.

If you have been eliminated for having refusals and you know that the most probable cause is overfacing, do not be too proud to enter a smaller class at the next show that you go to. Even if you have to jump *hors concours* in a Novice class, most shows will be more than happy to accommodate you. They may even allow you to jump *hors concours* in the jump-off too.

What happens if I have a fall?

Unfortunately, occasionally you will have a fall. Current BS and FEI rules state that if you fall off you are eliminated and you must leave the arena. Obviously if you or your horse is injured in the fall, you should not attempt to jump again in the collecting ring. If you are not injured it would seem sensible however, to attempt to regain your horse's confidence straight away. Having ascertained that your horse has not been injured in any way, you can take him into the collecting ring and jump four or five small fences to renew his confidence. Keep the fence low and narrow to start with, but try to raise it to a height comparable with the fence you fell at, before you finish. If you can enter another, similar height class, in the same arena, all the better. The fall may have been apparently innocuous, but horses do remember falls for a long time, particularly if they have hurt themselves and, if the fall frightened you, you can rest assured that it frightened your horse even more.

Ooops! Well it does happen.

At the end of the day…

If you are riding your own horse at a show, the most important thing to remember is that you are not there to please your parents, your groom or your coach – you are there to please yourself.

Whether you have won or lost, at the end of the day you will need to hold a brief review of your rounds. Have you achieved your goal? Have you improved your performance? If problems occurred, do you know why and do you think you can prevent them from happening again?

If problems have occurred, don't be tempted to abandon your system or completely change your training. However, if you can detect flaws in the plans you have made and can think of ways of improving them in future, you will have made a positive step to improving your skills. (That said, if you have been doing the same things for a period of time and the system is definitely not working, look at the whole thing objectively and see what you need to change, or get some fresh advice.)

Always look at the positives. What did you like about the round? There is always something good to reflect on, so use that to think about what you can do to improve the next round. Horses are horses and we cannot predict their every move, nor should we get aggravated by them just because they have a bad day. There is always another day and another show.

If you are lucky enough to have won the competition remember it is not 'you', who have won, but you and your 'team'. Thank your horse, groom, friends, family and your coach. Also remember to thank the organisers, including the judges and the collecting ring steward. A little courtesy goes a long way.

GUY WILLIAMS

"It is important to work hard and never give up; to have great horses, great owners, good facilities and a very understanding wife."

One of the hardest-working riders on the circuit, Guy has been Great Britain's No.1 rider, a valuable and reliable team member and a winner of the Hickstead Derby.

More Advanced Jump Training

B Y 'MORE ADVANCED', I am referring to Foxhunters and beyond – hopefully the reasonably talented show jumper's second and third years. By this stage your horse's *rhythm, impulsion, tempo* and balance should be well established; he should be familiar with jumping in first round and jump-off situations, on all terrains and in all weathers at Novice level, and is now ready to move on to bigger and better things.

Jumping bigger fences

What is it that makes it more difficult to achieve success over bigger and wider fences? The one thing that puts most people off tackling the bigger competitions is their own perceived lack of ability. Most people have more ability than they think they have and often their horses have less ability than their owners think.

Not every horse sold as a 'show jumper' is going to be capable of jumping enormous tracks, yet most people who go out and buy a 'show jumper' believe that they can. The realisation that any one horse is not going to become an internationally renowned Grand Prix performer can be painful for both owner and horse. A horse who is constantly faced with jumps that are at the limit of his scope, or even beyond it, will become frightened, sore and resentful. Eventually he will throw in the towel and will refuse habitually, nap or even refuse to enter the arena at all. Yet, if the same horse is allowed to continue jumping at a height at which he feels comfortable, he could give somebody years of pleasure as a schoolmaster.

There is no tangible way of knowing how high your horse can jump, other than stepping into the unknown, gradually introducing him to bigger and bigger courses. Only you or your coach will be able to tell whether or not your horse is comfortable and capable of answering these bigger questions.

Training technique over bigger fences

Throughout your horse's training you should gradually introduce first wider and then higher fences. You can easily introduce wider fences coming out of a combination, within a grid, or at the end of a related distance. It is important that you don't ask your horse to lengthen his stride coming into the wider fence. Indeed, you need to slightly shorten his stride. This will give you an indication of whether your horse is confident enough to open out and jump the wider fences. I prefer to use a double, with a one- or two-stride distance, or a related three-stride distance, with the oxer as the second element, to test the horse and to encourage him to open himself out over the fence.

Once you have ascertained that your horse is capable of jumping a wider fence, you need to find out whether or not he can also jump higher. Using the same combination, grid or related stride as you have done previously, close the oxer right up, perhaps to just a 30cm (1ft) spread, lower the front rail and raise the back rail higher than you would normally jump. For example, if you are comfortable jumping 1.10m (3ft 7in), then raise the back rail to 1.20m (4ft) or even 1.30m (4ft 3in). This will give the horse a chance to back off the front rail and reduce the chance of running into the fence and getting a fright.

Don't raise any fence more than 5cm (2in) at a time; this way the fence does not become too daunting too quickly. Always try to ensure that you have a friend or assistant on the ground when you are widening or increasing the height of fences, so that fluency is maintained. In any one session you could raise the fences by 5 cm (2in) up to seven times. The rider's most important role is to keep meeting these fences at exactly the same speed, in exactly the same rhythm, absorbing the increase in height.

This exercise will test your power of self-control, more than your horse; inevitably, if you are inexperienced, it is you who will run out of courage and confidence, before the horse. As soon as you begin to see the fence getting high, you will begin to think 'Gallop'; as soon as you do this, your horse will run on to the forehand, and as soon as he does so you will have lost the battle for control. Think *power* not speed.

Keeping within the discipline of the double combination or the related distance, you will not meet the second element on a bad stride – given that you have approached the first element on a good stride! Make sure that the fence going into the combination is not so big that it causes you or your horse stress, and that it is not so small that it does not prepare your horse for what is to come. Your 'placing fence' should allow you to glide to the second, more testing fence.

Don't try to get the height and width at the same time, as to do so would be more likely to cause problems than to find answers. Once you have ascertained that your horse can jump wider and higher fences than you thought him capable of, you can begin to fit wider and higher fences into your training courses at home.

A note of caution here: now that you know your horse can jump wider and higher than you thought he could, don't be tempted to go out and try to prove it at a show straight away. Having jumped good double-clears in the Beginner and Novice classes, do not suddenly be tempted try the Intermediate or Advanced classes.

I am a great believer in the idea that your horse should be able to jump 10cm (4in) higher at home, on a regular basis, than he needs to jump in the ring, particularly at the Novice levels. Obviously, once you get above the Novice levels and your horse is jumping well at home, then the amount of jumping that you do at home will be reduced, not increased. As long as he is jumping comfortably at home the height and width he will be expected to clear in any jump-off situation, you should feel that you are doing enough.

Always make sure that it is the second element of any related distance that is the bigger of the two fences. If you were to make the first element of a related distance the larger of the two obstacles, then any mistake you make at that fence will be magnified by the time you reach the second obstacle, leading to *big* problems!

Power, not speed

I would reiterate here that, to jump bigger fences, you will need more power, not more speed. Once you have developed the skill of producing power in your horse's stride, by keeping him contained between the hand and leg aids, then you can begin to cope with bigger fences. However, remember that the speed at which you approach upright fences will not be the same speed at which you approach spread fences. You need a little more power and speed as you approach spread fences and you need more accuracy as you approach upright fences. At no time must you gallop flat out at fences but you must learn to ride at a slightly faster, stronger pace, as you will be expected to do so all the time once you begin to enter the upper grade competitions.

Dealing with different types of fence

As you enter the Intermediate stage of show jumping, you will start to face treble combinations. Do not put your horse off by trying to jump huge treble combinations at home, but keep them low so that your horse maintains his confidence when he meets treble combinations in the ring. The last thing that you want is a horse who is frightened and seeking ways to avoid jumping.

You are also going to come across ditches, water jumps, dykes and banks. Your aim should be to introduce your horse to all of these different obstacles in a schooling situation before he comes across them in the competition arena. I jump

POINTS TO PONDER... Impulsion works for you; speed works against you.

my young horses over small ditches and water jumps from a very early age, so that when they come across these spooky things at a later date, I hope they are not fazed by them. Do not *assume* that your spooky, flighty horse is going to have a big problem with ditches and waters – some of the hottest horses I have owned have taken to these obstacles like ducks to water and yet some of the slowest and calmest of horses have hated the idea of going near a hole in the ground – perhaps they were worried that I might bury them there!

'Natural' obstacles

Water obstacles

Start by introducing your horse to water trays. This can either be a narrow wooden tray painted blue, a blue tarpaulin or even a split, blue plastic fertiliser bag, held down securely with poles. If your horse approaches and jumps the water tray as if he has been jumping them all his life and he clears it out of his stride, you are unlikely ever to have problems. If he spooks a little bit, runs past or stops a couple of times but is then willing to jump the tray and then jumps it with more and more confidence, once again you are unlikely to have problems in the future.

The difficult horse is the one with whom you spend the entire morning trying to get him near the tray and the entire afternoon trying to get him over it and then he does exactly the same thing the next day, the day after and the day after that. My own feelings are that, if after five or six days, the horse still does not want to know, you have problems that may prove insurmountable. True, you may in time at least get the horse over the obstacle, but you are unlikely to ever be able to trust him in a competition situation, where he will quickly learn that, if you cannot get him over the tray within three attempts, he does not have to have another go.

Water trays or 'Liverpools', should be introduced as early as possible because they are a common addition to any course from 1m (3ft 3in) upwards.

Ditches

At home, I use a lunge line and an experienced, calm helper to get my horses used to ditches. I will attach the lunge line to the horse in the same manner that I lunge – through one bit ring, over the poll and attached to the other bit ring. Then I will walk with the horse up to a small ditch, step over the ditch myself and stand on the landing side with the horse standing on the take-off side. It is now up to my helper to coax the horse to step over the ditch himself. This means that the helper uses the voice and the lunge whip gently against the horse's hocks. Very quickly the horse is likely to put in a prodigious leap over the gulf. Obviously I, standing on the landing side, have to be pretty quick-witted so as not to be squashed beyond recognition, but the horse will give warning that he is about to take the plunge. For this exercise to be successful and safe, the ditch used must have guard rails on either side to prevent the horse from running out and to stop the lunge rein from snagging.

When he has jumped the ditch and you have given him plenty of pats and praise, you can start the process over again. Once your horse has learnt that the troll in the ditch is not going to leap out and grab him by the legs, he will find the whole process a great deal of fun. As he gains confidence you can jump him over the ditch whilst lungeing him on a circle, before jumping the ditch from his back. You can use the same procedure for jumping small water jumps and small banks.

Notes on introducing natural obstacles

If the horse is allowed time to see and understand the problem or the new challenge then he is more likely to be confident. Horses like to see clearly where they are going and to see the obstacle clearly. They also like to sniff and smell it, then they like to look over the top of the obstacle, so just think of eyes, nose and neck.

The important rules for jumping natural obstacles are:

- Start small and simple.
- Make sure there is someone on the ground to help you and to reassure your horse.
- Jump as many different obstacles in as many different surroundings as you can.
- Be progressive.
- The more confidence and experience your horse has gained outside the arena, the more confidence he will have inside the arena.

Ask your local show centre if you can come and school over their natural obstacles on a non-show day; most are willing to hire out their facilities. If possible, take your trainer with you to give you some help through any crisis to keep you level-headed. If you cannot take your trainer, be sure to take an experienced helper.

In years gone by, a season's hunting was almost obligatory for young show jumpers and this introduced them to a huge variety of natural obstacles. It also taught them to move on boldly and to attack their fences. Sadly, hunting is not what it was and the hunting ban has restricted a lot of the traditional practice of riding across country. There is also the value of modern show jumping horses to be taken into consideration – not too many owners want to risk their very valuable horses in the hunting field.

Jumping different obstacles in the arena

Having accustomed your horse to ditches, banks and water fences it is now time to put him to the test in the arena. This will be a little daunting initially but we are fortunate that today, most outdoor show centres offer Novice Derbys, in which the obstacles are quite small and straightforward. As you progress you will come across different obstacles but most of them will follow a certain formula.

The devil's dyke

Probably the most famous of all the Derby fences and certainly the trickiest, this requires a bold approach. It consists of three vertical fences, usually a stride apart. The ground slopes down from the first fence to the middle fence (which will have a ditch under it) and then upwards to the final fence. A devil's dyke is often approached too slowly, giving the horse time to look into the dyke and balk. It needs to be approached on a short, bold, forward stride with your horse collected well between your hands and legs. Ride the last few strides as if you mean to get through, not with a backward-thinking attitude. If your horse is unsure of himself, the last thing he needs is for you to feel unsure too.

   At the beginning you will have to risk the chance of dropping a pole off the first fence, for the sake of getting all the way through, but I am definitely *not*

In order to jump out of the devil's dyke well you must jump in well with speed, balance and confidence.

advocating galloping blindly through. Rather, you must gather up your horse's impulsion between hands and legs and ride him forward towards the dyke, not allowing him to become flat and loose. You must ride just as boldly through the second and third elements as you have to the first. Remember that, because of the upward slope, the fence out is going to be bigger than the fence coming in and the distance to the fence will seem longer, for the same reason. Don't worry about the slope going down to the middle fence – that is not a *horse* problem, it is a perceived *rider* problem. Your horse's momentum will carry him perfectly down to the second element, as long as you have ridden him well into the first. Beware though; he may balk at the ditch, so keep your head up, your seat down and ride with legs firmly around the horse's sides.

The water jump

These jumps are designed to test your horse's ability to jump width and his boldness to jump over water. Contrary to public opinion, you do not have to gallop flat out at a water jump to clear it! Nor do you need to canter to it too slowly and, whatever you do, do not try to find a perfect stride from which to take off.

Get your horse into that good, balanced, forward-thinking stride, held completely between your hands and your legs, and then don't hesitate. Whatever you feel, keep going and 99 times out of 100 you will arrive at the fence in an acceptable place from which to take off. My theory is that my horse needs to get to the fence a fraction before I do. If I am a split-second behind him, coming to the water, I am less likely to get an early bath. Like most people of any age, I have had one or two of those. There is nothing more uncomfortable than getting back into the saddle with soggy breeches and boots full of water.

The easiest way of getting your horse over water jumps in the arena is to have

This is the way we would all love to jump a wide water jump. Note the height the horse is making and so the width of the water is not such a problem.

made sure that he is fully at ease with getting over them at home, as discussed earlier this chapter. It is also important that your horse is quite comfortable in and around water. At one time show jumpers were loathe even to get their horse's feet wet, in case it taught them bad habits and they would not then try their hardest to clear the whole jump. I prefer my horses to understand that water won't harm them. I will happily ride my horses through puddles, streams, lakes and even into the sea, increasing their knowledge and decreasing their fears. It is easy to ride to a water jump when your horse is taking you there willingly, but virtually impossible if he is not. Most horses who refuse to jump water have been frightened by it at some time.

The double of water ditches or a double of dry ditches

This is really another step in the water jump saga. If your horse is confident jumping over water and is confident jumping double or treble combinations, then a pair of water ditches should cause you no problems. You should be able to ride to the ditches confidently, just as you would to ordinary double combinations. Set your canter up and remember to be a fraction of a second behind your horse; also remember to keep a good contact on your horse's head as you approach the ditches. If you get in front of your horse's movement, or allow him to drop his head to peer into the ditches, you are likely to be deposited at his feet, probably coming to rest in the ditch itself!

The Derby bank

Here is a perfect descent down a steep Derby bank: the horse has jumped off two-thirds the way down and landed in perfect balance to go on and jump the 1.60m (5ft 3in) vertical two strides away. (Note the rider's immaculate leg position.)

Derby banks come in all shapes and sizes – the ultimate is the one we have all seen on television, the Hickstead Derby bank, built by Douglas Bunn at 'The All England Show Jumping Course'. I rather suspect that not many of you will ever experience the thrill of travelling down the steep face of that bank. Even to stand at the edge of it and look down is a daunting sight and the first trip down it is quite frightening!

A less than perfect descent but a brilliant recovery. Never give up!

However, you will almost certainly come across some type of bank in your jumping career, most of which will be quite shallow. Banks are not there to be crawled down but to be ridden down strongly. Riding downhill is easier than most people think. Horses, generally speaking, do not fall head over heels as soon as they encounter a downward slope – they will balance themselves beautifully, as long as their rider keeps still and does not interfere with their balance. Remember that your horse's balance is not static – it is dynamic – and your job is to sit in the centre of that balance so that your weight doesn't affect him adversely.

When your horse travels downhill you should let your shoulders come forward, allowing your weight to move slightly forward, thus keeping your weight in the middle of your horse and off his quarters. This doesn't mean that you come forward of the horse's movement, because you keep your legs in a strong, forward position. If you allow your lower legs to slip backwards then you will put too much weight on your horse's shoulders, will become ahead of his action, will lose your balance (probably causing your horse to lose his) and will almost certainly reach the bottom of the slope before your horse!

If there is a fence at the bottom of the bank then you will need to be travelling at the right speed to jump it – you will also have to meet it in a balanced canter. Your horse will already be well on his hocks, having come down the bank, and will be ready to jump. If you are cantering downhill you will find, amazingly, that your horse will maintain his own rhythm. You would be hard-pushed to make any horse go quicker running downhill, as even the fizziest one will slow himself down to a sensible rate. When going down a steep bank it is, however, very important to keep the horse straight because if he becomes crooked he will be certain to lose his balance and rhythm.

As long as you can balance yourself and your horse, you can canter down the steepest slope. Many years ago the Italian Cavalry, the *Tore de Quinto*, used to carry out an exercise in which a whole troop would canter their horses down what appeared to be an almost vertical slope, in a classical, Caprilli seat. Anyone who fell off probably had to muck out the whole stable for a year, yet they were unlikely to come off, because no horse will ever go faster downhill than he wants to!

The same rule applies to the table or road jump as to the devil's dyke – jump on with confidence and ride off with flair.

Tables

Those who compete in horse trials may understand tables in cross-country parlance as being broadly similar in construction to a picnic table. However, in the context of show jumping, the term describes a different obstacle. Sometimes called a 'road crossing' (or even, for some obscure reason, a 'tennis court'), a show jumping table usually consists of a jump of perhaps 1m (3ft 3in) up onto a raised surface, then three to four strides on the raised bank to a jump back to the ground.

These don't usually cause too much of a problem, but again you must remember to approach them boldly. If you jump on to and off them boldly, you should have no difficulties. Don't worry about how you land – the drop is no greater than that of jumping an ordinary fence of the same height. In other words,

A table, sometimes called a road crossing

if the height of the table is 1m (3ft 3in) and the drop is 1.30m (4ft 3in), then it is no different from jumping a fence that is 1.30m (4ft 3in) high, so do not let the drop trouble you.

If there is a ditch in front of, or behind the table, you must approach it with the same attitude as you might do when approaching a ditch before or after an ordinary fence – boldly and in balance.

Saddlery and Equipment

TRAINING YOUR HORSE CORRECTLY involves training him in the equipment that suits him best. That is not necessarily a snaffle bit and a cavesson noseband. If your horse has a delicate mouth, he may not like the nutcracker action of the snaffle and may work better in a straight-mouthed bit. Some horses are calmed by the effect of the curb chain, yet some are excited by it. It is the responsibility of you and your trainer to ensure that you are bitting your horse for comfort and control. One rule does apply in every circumstance: tack must fit correctly; a tight curb chain will irritate and block the forward movement; a bit which is too small will pinch and a bit which is too wide will rub. There are many different scenarios, so take advice from an experienced professional.

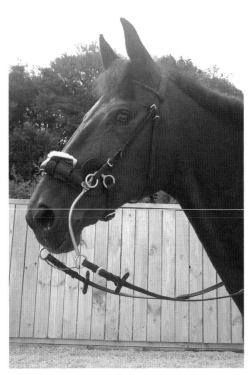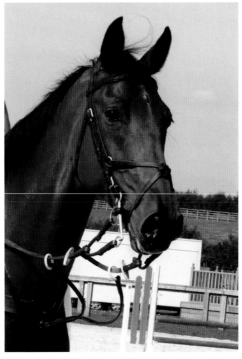

It is important to find out what bitting arrangement suits the individual horse. Here, a hackamore and a Pelham with a Grackle noseband.

Show jumping saddles are now mainly close-contact models that are light and very comfortable for both horse and rider. However there are some riders who prefer a deep-seated, general-purpose saddle; these saddles do give a less experienced or less well-balanced rider a degree of confidence. General-purpose saddles tend to have deeper panels, larger saddle flaps and more pronounced knee and thigh rolls.

Because the majority of shows are now held on artificial surfaces, the need for studs is far less than it used to be. I would still like to see more show jumping on grass but progress is what it is and prepared artificial surfaces are the future, so I suspect that grass field shows may eventually die out altogether. But because we do still jump on grass, we do need to understand the reason for studs and how to fit them.

Front tendon boots are a must for every jumping horse. It is just not worth the risk of jumping without them. Rear boots are optional and may depend on the horse's action. Bell boots or overreach boots are again optional and have largely died out, but many riders still swear by them and it is just personal preference.

School Aids and Gadgets

CHAPTER 24

Shortcuts or just plain laziness?

SOME TIME AGO I was given a cylinder weighing about 2kg (4lb 6oz). It had clips attached to each end. Apparently this dead weight was to be clipped to either side of a poor horse's bit and its aim was to lower the horse's head. More probably the horse's head would shoot up as soon as the weight was removed, out of pure relief! This sort of contraption is pure marketing hype, more likely to cause harm than good.

I do not have a problem with people using most training aids and auxiliary reins; what I do have a problem with is people using those aids or reins when they aren't skilled enough to do so properly. This can be not just foolish but downright cruel. Schooling aids, in the wrong hands, are a bit like a cutthroat razor in the hands of a monkey.

During my career with horses I have used nearly every training aid in the book. Most I have discarded almost immediately, some I have used to advantage for periods of time and a few I have used to great advantage over a number of years. The two fundamental points to consider are:

- Does the horse actually need the aid?
- Does the rider understand the aid's function and use?

I have often thought that the people most qualified to use schooling aids are those least likely to do so.

Training aids should not be used on very young horses. Young horses should be allowed to develop their musculature, balance and strength in a natural way. Using artificial aids on a horse who isn't ready, either physically or mentally, is asking for trouble in the long term. Another important point to remember is that, unless your horse is moving with impulsion and away from your leg, the use of any additional rein or artificial aid is futile.

Before you ride or lunge your horse in any form of artificial aid ask yourself the following questions:

- Are you experienced enough to cope if something goes wrong?
- Have you studied your horse's temperament and considered whether he is going to be able to cope with the pressures he is going to be put under?
- What is his conformation like – can he physically do what is required?
- Are you going to overstress him in a serious way by trying to force issues that should be left until the horse is fully fit?
- Have you taken good advice from somebody who really knows how these things work?
- Can you do the same job without the aid you are intending to use?
- Are your skills great enough to enable you to carry on the work of the aid once you have removed it?
- Do you *really* need to use an artificial aid?
- Now that you have answered all the questions above, have you been honest with yourself?

The final point to remember is that no training aid is there to force a horse into a particular shape; it is there to develop that shape. If you have been to a gymnasium to try to develop your own muscles, you will know that this takes time. If you force yourself to work too hard for too long, you end up with pulled muscles and strained ligaments – in other words a lot of pain for no gain! It is seldom necessary to use any aid for longer than 30 minutes at a time.

Some useful training aids

In addition to the devices mentioned below, the Pessoa system and the Chambon are undoubtedly useful training aids, but their use is restricted to work on the lunge and since they have already been covered in Chapter 4 they are not mentioned further here. Draw reins can, however, be used both when lungeing and riding and, since their form of use varies somewhat between the two situations, it is covered both in Chapter 4 and below.

Martingales

Martingales, if fitted correctly, can be a great deal of help in the arena. Unfortunately, incorrectly fitted martingales are seen all too often, restricting the horse's action to a point at which he is unable to jump or move correctly or effectively. Martingales *should* prevent the horse from getting his head above the point of control – they should not 'tie' his head down in a fixed position. In time the horse will learn to set himself against any badly fitting martingale and will become stiff and hollow.

The standing martingale

This runs from the girth through a neckstrap and attaches to a cavesson noseband. There has, for many years, been a rumbling debate as to whether standing martingales are restrictive during a jump or not: I think that they don't restrict the horse's jump, provided they are correctly fitted. The FEI does not permit standing martingales in the show jumping ring but the BS rules do. There should be no problem about using a standing martingale in the ring, provided it is not so tight that it interferes with the horse's shape during the jump. It is a very useful, humane aid that does not interfere with the bars of the horse's mouth in the same way as a badly fitted running martingale does.

When fitted correctly, you should be able to lift the martingale strap into the horse's gullet when he is holding his head in a correct position. You should also be able to get a vertical hand between the neckstrap and your horse's withers. In this position the standing martingale will not have any effect on the horse, unless he tries to throw his head up beyond a point of control. When used correctly the standing martingale will help the green, unschooled horse to maintain a steadier head-carriage and will act as a steadier 'pair of hands' for the less experienced rider.

How to measure and fit a standing martingale.

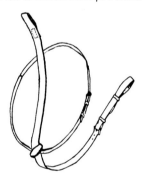

The martingale loop should be one hand's breadth from the horse's cheek.

The correctly fitted standing martingale; standing martingales should only be fitted to cavesson nosebands.

How to measure and fit a running martingale.

Fit rubber stops for safety – they prevent the martingale becoming tangled with the rein billets.

The martingale rings should be one hand's breadth from the horse's withers.

The Ernest Dillon precision rein action, both on the flat and over fences, is simply to create a correct contact whereby the rider can feel that the length of rein is constant and will therefore help the rider's 'muscle memory'.

The running martingale

This runs from the girth to a neckstrap (fitted as above), at which point it divides and is then attached to each rein by a ring. Rubber or leather rein stops must be used with the running martingale, to prevent the martingale rings becoming ensnared with the bit end of the reins, although this is less likely to happen using the more modern, loop-ended reins. If fitted correctly, with the two rings being able to reach the horse's crest, the running martingale will have no effect on the horse until he throws his head up beyond a point of control. Yet, as with the standing martingale, it is all too often fitted too tightly and pulls down on the bars of the horse's mouth, causing discomfort and a bad jumping style.

The Ernest Dillon precision rein

I developed this rein as a training aid to accustom riders to riding with their reins at the correct length. They are not, strictly speaking, a gadget, just a means of maintaining a constant, precise and correct contact. The concept is simple: the rein has adjustable loops on it by which the coach will set the length of rein. The adjustment will be set according to the length of the horse's neck and the rider's arms. Eventually the rider will realise how short the rein needs to be and how much leg is required to ride the horse initially to the rein and eventually through the rein, without setting the hands or tensing the forearm muscles or elbows, and so the need for gripping the reins too tightly will disappear.

In time muscle memory will take over and the rider will automatically ride with the correct rein length and with a precise contact. The horse will gradually become lighter and more 'uphill' and give a more athletic feel. Over a fence, with the precision rein, the follow-through will be automatic and, again, will develop a confidence in the contact.

These reins are only of use on the flat and over show jumps; they are not to be used with cross-country obstacles, as the occasional need to slip the reins on a cross-country course is not possible with the rein's loops.

The reins have also had good results for riders who have any arthritic or rheumatoid issues.

Side-reins and the Harbridge

As discussed in the earlier text on lungeing, side-reins are two adjustable reins that will either have a short, elasticated section or will have a rubber ring inserted along each length, to allow some measure of 'give' within the rein itself. They are attached at one end to the rings of the bit and at the other end to the girth, under the saddle flaps. They are used to keep the horse's head in a correct position whilst on the lunge. Initially you should fit them so that they are just taut whilst the horse is relaxed, but aren't pulling his head in towards his body. There is no quick-release mechanism for side-reins (or the Harbridge) and if the horse takes a dislike to them there is a fair chance that he may career backwards at speed or rear up, so be careful. Once the horse is used to feeling the action of the side-reins they can gradually be tightened until the horse's nose is in a vertical line with his ears. It is the job of the person lungeing the horse to ensure that the horse moves forward into the side-reins and does not tuck his head in to avoid their action, or lean heavily on the reins. If not used correctly, side-reins will produce a horse who is stiff and backward-thinking.

Show jumpers often use side-reins attached to the girth, under the horse's belly, coming out between his forelegs. The reason for this is that it encourages the horse to maintain a lower head-carriage than in ordinary side-reins. This arrangement is nowadays known as the Harbridge. Again, used correctly, it can have some beneficial effect on the way some horses carry themselves. I do not advocate the use of the Harbridge or side-reins whilst riding, for obvious safety reasons but, as with all things used correctly and with caution, experienced professionals can use their own judgement.

POINTS TO PONDER...

There is a mouth at the end of the reins.

Draw reins and running reins

'Just chuck 'im in draw reins, that'll pull 'is 'ead in!'…a statement I hate to overhear but one that I do, too frequently. Draw reins are *not* intended to *pull* the horse's head in. Their purpose is to encourage the horse to carry his head and neck in a low, flexed manner in which he can engage his quarters and work over his back and through his body. Correctly employed, draw reins will encourage correct development and musculature but they should not be used on young horses as a matter of course.

Draw reins, when used correctly, should not be tight or restrictive.

Draw reins should only be used when all attempts to create a correct shape have failed. They are a useful aid in the re-schooling of horses who have developed bad habits, such as the horse who is 'running through' the bridle with his jaw crossed and his head in the air. A few sessions in draw reins will put this horse back on the right road and will give him an idea of what is expected of him. Draw reins are also useful for the horse who refuses to flex through the withers and the poll, provided there is no anatomical reason for this problem. They will also assist flexion by encouraging the horse to lower his head and neck on to a longer rein, but you must be careful not to force things. If a horse has been carrying himself in a particular way for a long time, then you can not instantly ask him to carry himself in a different way altogether.

Running reins act in the same way as side-reins to help the rider achieve a more 'uphill' outline, but again there should be no pulling action.

Draw reins can also be useful when you are teaching a horse to change the leading leg in canter. They do eliminate some of the obvious resistances and evasions incurred when the horse is trying to understand the flying change. So often in these circumstances, the horse will 'run through' the bridle – draw reins will minimise the risk of this evasion becoming an obstacle in the way of progress.

Draw reins can be fitted in two ways: they can either be attached to the girth between the horse's legs or to the girth straps under the rider's knees, they then pass through the bit and go straight to the rider's hands. Using the latter method, the reins are better known as 'running reins'. The show jumper usually prefers to work with the 'draw rein', as the show jumping horse needs to work in a lower outline than a dressage horse. Bending and stretching are the two key elements in developing the horse's top line muscles. The show jumper is continually trying to develop the muscles that the horse uses to jump, so it makes sense to work in that shape.

When draw reins are being used correctly the reins will be loose, as the horse has accepted the pressure of the reins by being ridden into them from the leg, and he will begin to realise very quickly that he can take the pressure away by himself as he accepts the action of the draw reins. When the horse becomes flexible and accepting, then the draw reins have no further use and become a preventative rather than an active aid. Only when the horse raises his head beyond the point of control will the action of the draw reins again come into play.

Running reins have a similar effect to draw reins but the horse's head will be carried slightly higher. Working a horse in running reins over a long period of time is likely to have a slight fixing effect on the horse's neck and, in time, he will find it easy to duck behind the reins and not go forward so well.

The Market Harborough and the Abbot-Davies balancing rein

Several reins have developed directly from the running or draw reins. Two that spring instantly to mind are the Market Harborough and the Abbot-Davies balancing rein.

The Market Harborough

The action of the Market Harborough is similar to that of the draw reins. The reins run between the horse's forelegs and through the bit rings but then attach to various points on the bridle reins, depending on how severe an action you wish to produce. The Market Harborough is allowed in National Senior competitions in the UK, as long as it is attached to a plain snaffle. Along with running and standing martingales, these are the only aids permitted in the arena.

Although the Market Harborough is allowed in the arena, I do not like to see it used by any but the most experienced riders. If the rider is out of balance it can have a dramatically bad effect on the way a horse jumps.

The Abbot-Davies balancing rein

The aim of the Abbot-Davies balancing rein is to create the correct musculature to assist the horse to carry himself in a correct manner. It has three working positions, the first of which actually uses the horse's tail. The rein is attached to the horse's tail using a stretchable rubber fitting, travels under his belly through pulleys attached to the bit ring and clips to the rein. This is intended to encourage greater engagement of the horse's hindquarters, thus working on both the front and back end of the horse. In the second position it attaches to the girth, again using the stretchable rubber fitting, runs through the pulleys and clips to the bridle reins and, in the third position, it is clipped to the poll. This third position is mainly used for lungeing.

The Abbot-Davies balancing rein should be the rein of choice for the less experienced rider, who may not be entirely balanced in the saddle and whose instinctive reactions are not quite as quick, if things go wrong, as a more experienced person. It also limits the pulling power of the rider's hands so that the rider can't be lazy with the leg aids.

The de Gogue

The de Gogue is a schooling rein derived from the Chambon, to be used while the horse is being ridden. It can be used in two positions.

- In the passive position, the rein passes from the girth to a ring at the breast, where the reins split into two. Each rein passes through a ring either side of the poll, through the bit rings and then returns to be clipped at the breast ring.
- In the active position, once the reins have passed through the bit rings, they travel directly to the rider's hands.

In the passive position the de Gogue can be used on the lunge in much the same manner as the Chambon. In the active position the rider can use the de Gogue and, because it is not fixed, the rider can release the action of the rein if the horse reacts adversely to its pressure. Both positions have much the same effect as the Chambon, working primarily on the horse's poll and, to a lesser extent, on his lips, encouraging him to lower his head and engage his quarters thus developing a strong top line.

The Bungee

I was given this rein, which originates in Poland, a few years ago. It is an elastic rein which goes from the girth through one bit ring, over the poll, through the other bit ring and returns to the girth. It has a similar effect as the Chambon but will give a little, if the horse becomes upset by the pressure on the poll; therefore it is a rein that is safe to ride in.

Keeping your Show Jumper

CHAPTER 25

Feeding

THERE ARE FAR TOO MANY OVERFED, overweight horses, trying to compete on the show jumping circuit. So often a horse's bad behaviour and lack of progress stems directly from inappropriate feeding. The reasons for this are many, but most stem from bad and outmoded methods of stable management. If you are 'fighting the feed bin' – that is, spending most of your time when riding trying to expend the excess energy that you have fed your horse – you are unlikely to make any progress, either at home or at shows. To see jumping ponies being lunged for upwards of half an hour before they have settled down enough to accept a rider is quite a common, but fundamentally unnecessary sight. Children's ponies do not need half a bucket of concentrates, three times a day – in fact this is truly bad for them. Most ponies will compete happily off grass and good hay. Many feed companies now run helplines to advise on correct feeding regimes; if you are not sure what to feed your horse, ring the experts!

Protein-rich feeds should not be given to show jumpers in large amounts; they tend to fare better on feeds high in fibre and carbohydrates, which will ultimately assist in muscle function. My horses have a considerable amount of fibre in their diets – in fact they have access to as much high-quality, dust-free hay or haylage as they want. Many people now wet hay as a matter of course, ridding the hay of dry spores harmful the horse's respiratory system. Haylage – the generic term for grass that is partially dried then vacuum-sealed – is becoming more commonly used as a dust-free alternative.

Whether you choose to feed hay or haylage, it is imperative that the food you choose is of the best quality. If you don't know what you are looking for, then make sure you have someone with you who does. Poor-quality fodder will at best, be of no benefit to your horse, and at worst, will cause him serious, permanent damage.

A well-equipped show jumping paddock, featuring an International set of show jumps.

What dreams are made of…
a beautiful, well-set-out stable
yard.

Well-fenced paddocks with good natural shade will keep your valuable horse safe in his down time.

A wash-down stall with a non-slip
floor and overhead hose with both
hot and cold running water.

A modern horse-walker with a roof.

This is just pure luxury at a certain
age. Note the well-appointed stable
block.

Fitness

Show jumpers do not have to push themselves to the extremes of physical exertion that other types of sports horses have to. Horses used purely for show jumping do not have to be 'racing' or even 'eventing' fit, the latter having to run pretty much as fast as they can for up to a quarter of an hour at a time. By contrast, a show jumper has to produce an extreme burst of energy, for an absolute maximum of three minutes of a time. That said, it will be evident that the show jumper must be sufficiently fit to do his job well, without 'running out of steam' – or jump.

Before you start to get your horse fit, check his resting heart rate, resting respiratory rate, his normal temperature and keep a record of them. These baseline observations will give you a physical indication of whether your horse is ever unwell. You will find that as your horse becomes fitter, his resting pulse and respiration rates will become slower.

To attain the degree of fitness necessary to compete you should first follow a simple fittening regime such as:

- A week at walk for half an hour a day.
- A week of walk for an hour a day.
- Two weeks of walk and trot for an hour a day.
- Two weeks of walk, trot and canter for upwards of an hour a day.

This is only necessary if the horse has had a prolonged holiday of say, six or eight weeks, or has clearly never been fit before. Once your horse has achieved this level of fitness you can maintain it through the everyday work that you do with him; alternating schooling on the flat with work over jumps, hacking out, competing and the occasional day off, enjoyed in the field. Remember, that to perform well, your horse has to be mentally as well as physically fit and variety is important, but this should not be confused with inconsistency. Horses are creatures of habit and like to know what is likely to happen to them, and when. Routine times for mucking out, feeding and riding will greatly reduce your horse's stress levels.

A two-week break, such as when you take your summer holiday, is unlikely to affect your horse's general fitness, as long as he is turned out or is allowed to stretch his legs on a horse-walker each day. If you have a break from riding that is longer than this, it may be necessary to start your fitness programme again, although not necessarily from the beginning.

Stable management

Most serious show jumpers are stabled through the year. It is possible to compete from the field but most riders do not have vast acreage and many feel that their horses concentrate on their jumping better if competed from the stable. Personally, I like my horses to spend as much of the summer in the paddock as possible, provided they do not become grossly overweight.

A thick, comfortable bed will encourage your horse to relax in his stable.

It is becoming more and more probable that you will use a rubber floor in your stables as an anti-slip surface and to some extent as insulation against the cold concrete or cement floor. However, I am not in favour of replacing a warm, comfortable bed with just rubber; it can be very dirty and can also emit an unpleasant odour when the ammonia mixes with the natural smell of rubber. If you are using a rubber floor, or a concrete floor, then the type of bedding you use is as important as the quality of fodder.

There are now many types of bedding to choose from and which one you use will depend on cost, availability, your method of disposal and your horse. Good quality wheat straw is cheap, relatively easy to find and usually you can entice the local mushroom grower into removing your muckheap for you. On the downside, some horses think that good quality wheat straw tastes really good and will gorge on it. The other downside is that, however good the quality of the straw, it will be host to fungal and mould spores which will, in time, affect the horse's respiratory system.

Shredded paper, dust-extracted shavings and shredded hemp are all popular. Dust-free bedding materials and rubber matting are now often used to dramatically reduce bedding bills in the long term. Rubber matting can be used completely on its own, although many people like to throw down a small amount of shavings to absorb splash and moisture from urine. Rubber stable floors are very common now, but I think that a rubber floor should be to provide a non-slip surface under a bed of straw or shavings, as opposed to being replacement bedding.

Whatever bedding you decide to use and whatever method of mucking out you employ – full mucking out once or twice a day, semi-deep litter or total deep litter – the same golden rules apply: the bed should be sufficiently deep that the horse cannot feel the underlying surface, and dry enough that he does not become damp when lying down.

A horse who is stabled should be ridden, or at least be able to stretch his legs somehow, at least once a day. The best method of achieving the latter is to turn him out into a safe, grassed paddock but if you have no grazing, then turning out into a schooling area or exercise on a horse-walker is totally acceptable. Horse-walkers are the boon of many big stables, enabling several horses to be exercised at one time.

Farriery

I am very aware that the modern farrier is as important as the vet and in fact a farrier's apprenticeship is almost as long as a vet's. It is, however, the rider's ultimate responsibility to make sure that the farrier is called at the right time. There is no clear-cut time-span after which the horse needs to have attention to his feet, but, as a rule of thumb, I would say not less than four weeks and not more than six weeks between visits. You will soon decide between your farrier and yourself what is necessary for your particular horse. The adage, 'No foot, no horse', is as relevant now as the day it was first coined many hundreds of years ago, and one thing is certain – no horse will jump at his best if he is uncomfortable in his feet, or unsure of his footing.

Physiotherapy, chiropractics and osteopathy

By its very nature, the sport of show jumping exerts all manner of stresses and strains on the equine athlete. It is important that we get the right team behind us and that should be a team we can trust. I have heard enough nonsense talked in relation to the way horses operate and what can go wrong in terms of physiology and biomechanics to fill a library. The one sure-fire thing is that if the person you are using has bona fide qualifications, is experienced in the treatment of horses and comes recommended by experienced horse people, then you should feel confident in seeking their opinion. A word of caution however – opinions in every walk of life differ greatly, so my general rule is to try to apply the laws of logic. If it *sounds* logical and sensible then follow your instinct. If it sounds too good to be true, then it usually is.

A solarium – a luxury in any yard.

Past Masters

I T HAS LONG BEEN MY BELIEF that to be successful in your chosen sport you should have knowledge of the history of the sport and know something of its past masters as well as its current superstars, both human and equine. In the show jumping world I am constantly disappointed by the apathy shown by some of our young riders to the history and past masters who shaped our great sport. These people were iconic in their achievements and, if you consider that they had little or no prior knowledge to refer to, they were the pioneers of the sport. As modern riders we owe them a huge debt of gratitude because, without these people, there would be no sport of show jumping as we know it today.

This last part of my book is an attempt to rectify this vacuum in some small way, and try to show how truly great the past masters were and how amazing were the horses they rode. I have also included current riders who, I believe, will go down in history as heroes and masters of their craft. I would like to add to stress that I have chosen just a few riders who, in my opinion, particularly influenced the modern-day sport, but I realise there were many hundreds more riders to whom we need to be eternally grateful: my choices are based on my own opinions and experiences.

UK riders

Pat Smythe OBE

What can I say about Pat Smythe? She was a true pioneer, a horsewoman, an ambassador, a writer of children's books, a gutsy and determined competitor and totally self taught.

Pat's first training ground was Richmond Park

Pat Smythe OBE

where she practised her technique jumping the park benches and tree trunks on a one-eyed Arab/Dartmoor pony called *Pixie*. I wonder what the health and safety people today would say about that? Her first real show jumping competition was in the Children's Jumping class at the Richmond Royal Show where she jumped four clear rounds to win.

Her first 'proper' horse came in the shape of the 15.2hh Thoroughbred *Finality*. She was asked to represent Great Britain at the age of 18; at 20 she won the Leading Jumper at the Horse of the Year Show and shared the Puissance with the 17.2hh *Foxhunter*, clearing the (in those days) imperial height of 6ft10in (2.08m). That was the start of her illustrious career with her most notable horses – the ex-racehorse *Prince Hal*, the difficult grey mare *Tosca*, followed by her Olympic ride *Flanagan* and the great winners *Mr Pollard*, *Nobbler* and *Brigadoon*.

She rode in 13 winning Nations Cup teams, was four times Ladies European Champion, eight times British National Champion, winner of the Queen Elizabeth Cup and was not only the first lady to ride in an Olympic show jumping event in 1956 at the Stockholm Games, but was a member, at the same Olympics, of the bronze medal winning team. She won Grands Prix in Rome, Paris, Aachen, Madrid, London, Lucerne, Palermo and many other prestigious international venues.

Pat retired from competition in 1963 but kept a high profile in the sport by serving for many years on the BSJA executive committee.

Peter Robeson

Peter Robeson was a horseman way ahead of his time. He was a great advocate of correct dressage and systematic cavalletti work in the preparation of the show jumping horse. Always a perfectionist he was, at the time, one of the most stylish riders in the world. His horses worked in simple snaffle bridles and loose running martingales or often, no martingale at all. He rode with a quiet effectiveness and superb balance which enabled his often very sensitive horses to trust him and give of their best. He achieved most of his successes on just two horses, *Craven A* and *Firecrest*, but rode in two Olympic Games on rides relatively unfamiliar to him, *Scorchin* (later to be the ride of Pat Smythe) and *Law Court*, a horse produced and ridden by Malcolm Pyrah. Taking on a 'catch' ride is some feat for any competitor in any competition, let alone an Olympic Games!

A man of outspoken views, Peter does not suffer fools at all. However, I have been privileged to have had numerous conversations with him and he is a mine of valuable information and solid, well-founded methodology. His idea is that

Peter Robeson.

a solid framework of flatwork and cavalletti work will give a perfect preparation for the young horse in terms of suppleness and fitness, and he believes that progressive early training will prepare the horse for a long and successful career. Peter may not have been the prolific winner of as many competitions as Broome and Smith but he was a first-class example of how to manage and produce young horses in the best classical way. He would not sacrifice his horse's confidence or well-being to win; he would rather jump a good round even if it was not a winning round.

David Broome CBE

David Broome.

David Broome was born in Wales; he has lived and maintained his stables at Mount Ballan Manor, Crick, near Chepstow in Monmouthshire for most of his life. It is now the very popular Wales and West Showground.

His hallmark as a rider was an unbelievable ability to ride forward on a short, active stride and to seemingly never break the rhythm. He had an inbuilt clock in his head and always knew where he was in terms of the time and position in a jump-off. The other great quality Broome had as a rider was to 'fit in' with the horse's style and temperament and not try to dominate. This is reflected in the vast number of different horses on whom he gained international success, never more apparent than when he won the World Championship in 1970 on the feisty *Beethoven*. (He once modestly told me that it was *Beethoven* who won him the World title, but I think David played a pretty big part!)

A truly prolific winner of championships and Grands Prix on a multitude of horses, he will go down in history as one of the UK's finest

David Broome CBE Major Achievements

Olympic Games
- 1960 Rome: individual bronze
- 1968 Mexico: individual bronze
- 1988 Seoul: equal 4th place on *Countryman*

World Championships
- 1960 Venice: individual bronze
- 1970 La Baule: individual gold
- 1978 Aachen: team gold
- 1982 Dublin: team bronze

- 1990 Stockholm: team bronze

European Championships
- 1961 Aachen: individual gold
- 1967 Rotterdam: individual gold
- 1969 Hickstead: individual gold
- 1977 Vienna: team silver
- 1979 Rotterdam: team gold
- 1983 Hickstead: team silver
- 1991 La Baule: team silver

FEI World Cup
- World Cup: Jumping League winner 1979/80

World Cup Qualifier wins
- 1978/1979 's-Hertogenbosch
- 1979/1980 Birmingham
- 1979/1980 Wien
- 1979/1980 Bordeaux
- 1979/1980 Amsterdam
- 1980/1981 Olympia (London)
- 1981/1982 Olympia (London)

- 1981/1982 Dublin
- 1983/1984 Amsterdam

Hickstead Derby
- 1966

King George V Gold Cup
- 1960
- 1966
- 1972
- 1977
- 1981
- 1991

International Grand Prix wins include:
- 1960 Dublin

- 1967 Dublin
- 1968 Dublin
- 1970 La Baule
- 1973 St. Gallen
- 1975 Olympia (London)
- 1975 Dublin
- 1979 Amsterdam
- 1979 Dublin
- 1980 Olympia (London)
- 1981 Spruce Meadows
- 1981 Horse of the Year Show (Wembley, London)
- 1983 Amsterdam

sportsmen. He won the European Championships in 1961, 1967 and 1969 and individual Olympic bronze medals in 1960 and 1968; the latter was won on one of his best-known horses, *Mr Softee,* on whom he was only two fences (8 faults) behind the gold medal position. In 1960 he was also voted BBC Sports Personality of the Year. He won the World Individual Championship in 1970 and in the same year was *Western Mail* Welsh Sports Personality of the year. He turned professional in 1973 and in 1978 he was part of the British team that won the World Championship. He won the King George V Gold Cup a record six times on six different horses between 1960 and1991; a record yet to be equalled. He enjoyed most of his success on Irish Sport Horses and said his favourite horse of all was *Sportsman.*

He remains active in the administration of the sport.

Harvey Smith

Harvey Smith.

One of North Yorkshire's most famous sons, Harvey Smith was David Broome's greatest rival in National competitions; some of their clashes were the stuff of legends. 'Broomie' with his calm rhythmical riding, his face impassive, and Harvey with his Yorkshire granite jaw stuck out with a fierce determination to win everything he entered. The word 'lose' did not figure in Harvey's vocabulary.

Starting his career on the small, short-striding *Farmers Boy* he bought at a sale for £40, this ex-builder went on to become one of show jumping's legends. He made his Nations Cup debut in Dublin, helping the British team to win the prestigious Aga Khan Cup on his £40 horse!

Although Harvey was a great championship rider he was also a prolific winner of individual competitions, both National and International. His style followed his manner and upbringing. He was tough and pretty dominant as a rider, always in total control, riding forward on a short, very active stride. Harvey's horses were never in any doubt about who was in charge.

His career was often controversial; in 1971 he was disciplined (overturned on appeal) after he gave a 'V sign' to the judges (in fact it was aimed at the private box of Duggie Bunn), following a near-perfect round which won him the British Show Jumping Derby for the second year in succession. He was so sure he would win again he did not bother to bring the cup back, which caused Bunn, Master of Hickstead, and Harvey to have words.

Caroline Bradley

Caroline Bradley, one of the UK's most talented lady riders, tragically had her outstanding career cut short when she sadly died of heart failure at the age of 37, during a horse show. She was a dedicated show jumping rider and a shining example of hard work and commitment to any aspiring young rider. In fact dedication is an understatement when attached to Caroline Bradley's name; she would start earlier and work later than any rider before or since, and her untimely death robbed the UK of a first-class horsewoman.

Caroline Bradley.

I met Caroline when we were both about 21 and I took any and every opportunity to watch and learn from her exceptional skill. She was always approachable and enjoyed talking about her sport and gave the most credit to her horses.

Like Peter Robeson before her she was a firm believer in correct preparation founded on correct work on the flat and structured cavalletti work. She had phenomenal successes on a variety of different horses from Thoroughbreds to Warmbloods and everything in between.

Caroline won the Queen Elizabeth II Cup twice, the Toronto Open Show Jumping Championship and was the second woman to win the Hamburg Jumping Derby. Her best horses were *Tigre* and *Marius*. In 1979 she was voted *Daily Express* Sportswoman of the Year.

She also bought the great grey horse *Milton* as a newly weaned foal and rode and trained him until her tragic death in 1983, when John Whitaker took over the ride: *Milton* went on to become the first show jumper to win a million pounds.

Caroline Bradley
Major Achievements

World Championships
- 1978 Aachen, team gold

European Championships
- 1979 Rotterdam, team gold
- 1973 Ladies European Championship Vienna, individual silver

Past masters from overseas

I have pondered long and hard about who I should include in this section. I decided that, although there have been many great riders from overseas, those I have included are those whom I think have influenced the sport the most. In fact not only influenced, but also inspired the future generations of show jumpers with their style and with the manner in which they conducted themselves in their sport. Many readers will disagree and others will see my point but, a little like a fantasy football team, we all have our opinions. The important thing about opinions is that whatever opinion you have, it is never wrong, just different!

Raimondo's Achievements

Olympic Games
- 1956 Individual silver
- 1956 Team silver
- 1960 Individual gold
- 1960 Team bronze
- 1964 Individual bronze
- 1972 Team bronze

World Championships
- 1956 Individual gold
- 1960 Individual gold
- 1966 Individual bronze

Olympic appearances spanned 1957–1976 inclusive

Piero's Achievements

Olympic Games
- 1956 Team silver
- 1956 Individual bronze
- 1960 Individual silver
- 1960 Team bronze
- 1964 Team bronze
- 1972 Team bronze

Olympic appearances spanned 1948–1976 inclusive

European Championships
- 1958 Individual silver
- 1959 Individual gold
- 1961 Individual silver
- 1962 Individual silver

Raimondo and Piero d'Inzeo (*Italy*)

I am going to use a little artistic licence here because I will write about these brothers as one. To separate them would be very difficult as their careers ran parallel and their achievements were legendary. Piero was born in Rome in 1923 and Raimondo two years later. They were taught to ride in the traditional 'Caprilli' method, by their father Carlo, an officer in the Italian cavalry. The brothers were, of course, extremely popular in their own country and it would be impossible to say who was the more successful. The World Championships and the Olympic Games were only run in the same year on two occasions, 1956 and 1960. In 1960 Raimondo won the gold medal in both, a record which is never going to be repeated, because these two events will never again be run in the same year.

Raimondo rode in 32 Nations Cup winning teams, Piero in 41. Their Grands Prix wins are almost too many to count. They rode Irish Sport Horses throughout their careers, the most famous being *The Rock, Posillipo, Merango, Easter Light, Bellevue* and *Uruguay*.

The d'Inzeo brothers had international jumping careers lasting from 1947 through to 1977 and were still producing young horses right into the mid 1980s.

The brothers Piero and Raimondo d'Inzeo.

Hans Gunter Winkler (*Germany*)

One of the true amateurs of the sport; born in 1926, Hans Winkler remains one of the most successful championship riders ever. His tally of five Olympic gold medals, winning both team and individual in 1956 then three team gold medals, a team silver and a team bronze is a supreme achievement.

He was a consummate horseman with his style firmly based on a deep understanding of dressage and how the horse works. His riding education was enhanced through team selection and took place at the headquarters of equestrian sport at Warendorf in West Germany.

His most famous horse was the great mare *Halla*, one of the best horses ever to look through a bridle. Others included *Torphy*, a horse he rode in 17 winning Nations Cup teams, *Romanus* and *Cornelia*. In total he rode on 37 winning Nations Cup teams.

Winkler's style was very precise and disciplined; his horses were totally obedient and trained to perfection. He retired from competition in 1986 at the age of 60, after a career spanning three decades. Members of a 45,000 strong audience, at the famous Aachen arena, gave him a standing ovation waving white handkerchiefs.

William Steinkraus (USA)

Born in 1925 in Cleveland, Ohio, Bill Steinkraus was the epitome of style and effectiveness. A product of American Hunter Seat Riding, as a child and young rider he was a prolific winner of Hunter classes both on the flat and over fences. As a teenager he was also a winner of National Equitation Championships (equitation riding is judged on style and performance over fences up to 1.30m/4ft 3in) and, in the opinion of many experts, he was one of the most artistic, stylish and effective riders that show jumping has ever seen. He is still a huge influence on modern-day American show jumping riders.

During the World War II Steinkraus was a serving officer in the Far East as a member of the USA Cavalry. He then joined the United States Equestrian Team (USET) in 1951 and five years later he was appointed as its captain, a position he held for two years.

Steinkraus was a pupil of the famous USET coach Bertalan de Nemethy who was a huge influence on the post-war international scene. The highly successful team toured Europe in the 1950s, '60s and '70s, winning over 70 Nations Cups. Bill Steinkraus rode in 39 of these winning performances on a number of very famous, mostly Thoroughbred horses: *Democrat, Riviera Wonder, Ksar D'Esprit, Sinjon, Snowbound, Main Spring* and *Bold Minstrel* are the horses Steinkraus nominates as his best and most consistent partners.

His most famous victory was with *Snowbound* at the 1968 Olympic Games in Mexico City over what was arguably the biggest show jumping course ever built. Second was Great Britain's Marion Mould (née Coates), on the 14.2hh pony *Stroller* and the bronze went to David Broome on *Mr Softee*.

After retiring from international competition in 1972, Steinkraus continued to influence American show jumping for many years as chairman of USET. During these years the American team won team gold at the 1984 Olympic Games in Los Angeles and the World Championships at Aachen in 1986.

Hans Gunter Winkler Major Achievements

Olympic Games
- 1956 Individual gold
- 1956 Team gold
- 1960 Team gold
- 1964 Team gold
- 1968 Team bronze
- 1972 Team gold
- 1976 Team silver

Olympic appearances spanned 1956–1976 inclusive

World Championships
- 1954 Individual gold
- 1955 Individual gold

European Championships
- 1957 Individual gold
- 1961 Individual bronze
- 1962 Individual silver
- 1969 Individual bronze

William Steinkraus Major Achievements

Olympic Games
- 1968 Individual gold
- 1972 Team silver

Pan American Games
- 1959 Team gold
- 1963 Team gold
- 1967 Team silver

King George V Gold Cup
- 1956
- 1964

Grand Prix successes include Aachen, New York, Harrisburg, Rotterdam, Ostend and many more.

Pierre Jonqueres d'Oriola.

Pierre Jonqueres d'Oriola Major Achievements
Olympic Games
• 1952 Individual gold
• 1964 Individual gold
• 1964 Team silver
World Championships
• 1953 Individual bronze
• 1954 Individual silver
• 1966 Individual gold
European Championships
• 1959 Individual silver

Pierre Jonqueres d'Oriola (*France*)

One of my boyhood heroes, d'Oriola was the trendsetter for the classic French style of forward riding. He rode in the two-point forward seat on what appeared to be no contact on the horse's mouth, obviously making the whole performance look much easier than it was. An uncanny ability to judge distance a long way from the fence and perfect balance were the hallmarks of this, one of show jumping's most successful riders.

Born in 1920, he was taught to ride before he could walk by his father, himself a great horseman. His international debut was in his country's post-war Nations Cup in Nice, in which d'Oriola was on the winning team as well as taking the prize for the best individual performance. That same year he appeared in successful Nations Cup teams in Lucerne, London and Ostend and also won the King George V Gold Cup and the Grand Prix in Ostend, not a bad start to an international career!

In fact, over his illustrious 20-year career, d'Oriola took a dozen different horses to the top, becoming one of the most prolific winners of the post-war era; he rode with sympathy, harmony and with a marked lack of gadgetry.

He rode on 20 winning Nations Cup teams but most amazing was his list of Championship medals. His top horses included *Marquiss 111, Aigonne, Ali Baba, Voulette, Arlequin, Dark Noe, Pomone* and *Lutteur B.* Most of these horses were Anglo/Arabs and Selle Français/Thoroughbred types.

Nelson Pessoa (*Brazil*)

Brazilian Nelson Pessoa, known as 'Neco', became one of the most important riders of all times, influencing, with his incomparable technique and style, world equestrianism as a whole. Nowadays one can say that Nelson Pessoa is to riding, what Pele was to football. Besides being an expert on tack, he is also a master horse psychologist.

Back in the 1950s, when Pessoa was young, equestrianism in Brazil was a sport little practised by civilians but extremely popular within the military: all the great names of the sport were officers of the Brazilian armed forces. Yet among the civilian population one name stood out – that of Nelson Pessoa.

While still a junior rider, Pessoa won important competitions on the national scene and took part in the International of Rio de Janeiro. Three years later he joined the Brazilian team in his first performance overseas, in the International of

Nelson Pessoa.

Buenos Aires, Argentina. During this tour, 'Neco' enjoyed his first International level victory, in Mar del Plata. In 1956 he took part in the Stockholm Olympic Games. Then, in 1961, came the big opportunity to move to Europe.

By this time, Pessoa was on his way to becoming a legend and he paved the way for a great number of Brazilian riders to follow in his footsteps to Europe, which was then at the core of world equestrianism. In Europe Pessoa's accurate techniques drew everyone's attention and he became known as 'The Wizard', so bewitching was his riding.

His most famous horses were *Huipil, Larramy, Miss Moet*, the wonderful little grey *Grande Geste* and the not so little *Vivaldi*. With *Miss Moet* he set a Puissance record outdoors in Paris in 1983, clearing 2.33m (7ft 7¾in). He also has the distinction of being the oldest winner of the Hickstead Derby, winning it in 1996 at the age of 60 years young!

Pessoa also stands out as a coach, guiding several teams in Europe, the Middle East and Brazil (which included helping the Brazilian team to achieve their first-ever Brazilian Olympic medal in Atlanta in 1996). Perhaps his greatest achievement as a coach though is to be behind the brilliant career of his son, Rodrigo Pessoa, World Champion in 1998, three times World Cup winner and Olympic Champion.

**Nelson Pessoa
Major Achievements**

- Two gold medals and one silver in the Pan American Games
- Seven times champion (a record) of the Hamburg Derby
- Three times winner of the Hickstead Derby
- European Champion 1966
- Winner of 150 Grands Prix in Europe
- Winner of over 100 Puissances
- Four times Brazilian Champion

What Comes Next?

CHAPTER 27

YESTERDAY WAS GREAT but it was yesterday – what of now and tomorrow? There are, of course, many, many riders competing at the present who will become icons of the sport, some sooner and some later.

The great Whitaker dynasty (UK) will be talked about for as long as the sport of show jumping is practised. John for his patient and modest approach to every horse he rides and his amazing temperament under pressure; Michael for his tenacity and unbelievable will to win at every level.

Nick Skelton (UK) will be remembered for his ability, second to none, to produce horses from Novice level to the very highest level of competition. He will also be remembered for his courage in coming back from suffering a broken neck to almost win an Olympic gold medal.

Peter Charles (UK) is super-cool under pressure and, as well as being a prolific winner, he has been a stalwart full-back for the Nations Cup team on many occasions.

Ben Maher (UK) is, in my opinion, a real up-and-coming superstar and combines every facet of a true modern-day show jumping rider. He has flair, style, determination and courage, combined with a modest, unassuming attitude. He is one of the sport's potential greats.

Overseas, the number of truly great stars is too numerous to mention them all, so I have picked just a few.

Michel Robert (France) is one of my true heroes. In 2009 at the age of 61, he won the Global Tour Final and the Top Ten Grand Prix rider's prize. He is a true horseman, having been successful in both Olympic show jumping and three-day eventing and is still one of the most natural stylists the sport will ever see.

Marcus Ehning (Germany) is every rider's rider. He is effective, stylish, determined, cool, unflappable, sympathetic and strong-minded. I could go on, but suffice to say he is a real natural show jumper with an uncanny understanding of the sport.

Michel Robert.

Eddie Macken (Ireland) was a forerunner of good style. As a young man he appeared out of Ireland as a polished young rider and just continued to improve. Twice a World Cup finalist he was also four times winner of the Hickstead Derby on the great *Boomerang*. Still competing at the highest level, he is an inspiration to ambitious horsemen of any age.

Ludger Beerbaum (Germany) is another fierce competitor who will not lie down and accept defeat. If he is out of the top ten in the world for a short time it will be because he is busy producing yet another star. He is a prolific champion and will be around for many years to come.

Beat Mändli (Switzerland) has turned style into an art form. No other rider appears to be going nowhere and yet is travelling at speed and shaving seconds off everywhere. He is an absolute pleasure to watch.

Beezy Madden (USA) is one of those lady riders in the mould of Caroline Bradley, Pat Smythe, Marion Mould and Liz Edgar. She is as tough as any man and, under pressure, as cool as a cucumber. She is one of the most prolific winning lady riders of the twenty-first century.

Eddie Macken.

The Last Word

HORSES WILL CONTINUE TO BE WELL BRED and training will continue to improve. Show jumping courses cannot get any higher or wider and the technical aspect of course design has probably gone as far as it can. The time aspect of riding courses has had a huge influence on how the courses are ridden. Grand Prix speed is 400m per minute and the course designers are now much less generous with their measuring wheel, taking the tightest lines possible.

So how will show jumping develop? The main areas of progress will be in the understanding of the physiology and biomechanics of the horse's body and the understanding of the psychology of the horse's mind. These things will always continue to improve and develop, along with the furthering of veterinary science. The important thing is that true horsemen and horsewomen use the new technology and science in a responsible and wise manner.

The last word is a very important one:
'That which is most important has changed the least.
The Horse'.

Happy show jumping.